▶ Narrating the Past through Theatre

Also by Michael Bennett

REASSESSING THE THEATRE OF THE ABSURD: Camus, Beckett, Ionesco, Genet, and Pinter

WORDS, SPACE, AND THE AUDIENCE: The Theatrical Tension between Empiricism and Rationalism

REFIGURING OSCAR WILDE'S *SALOME* (*editor*)

EUGENE O'NEILL'S ONE-ACT PLAYS: New Critical Perspectives (*co-editor*)

palgrave▸pivot

Narrating the Past through Theatre: Four Crucial Texts

Michael Y. Bennett

palgrave macmillan

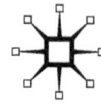

NARRATING THE PAST THROUGH THEATRE
Copyright © Michael Y. Bennett, 2013.

All rights reserved.

First published in 2013 by
PALGRAVE MACMILLAN®
in the United States—a division of St. Martin's Press LLC,
175 Fifth Avenue, New York, NY 10010.

Where this book is distributed in the UK, Europe and the rest of the world,
this is by Palgrave Macmillan, a division of Macmillan Publishers Limited,
registered in England, company number 785998, of Houndmills,
Basingstoke, Hampshire RG21 6XS.

Palgrave Macmillan is the global academic imprint of the above companies
and has companies and representatives throughout the world.

Palgrave® and Macmillan® are registered trademarks in the United States,
the United Kingdom, Europe and other countries.

ISBN: 978-1-137-27543-1 EPUB
ISBN: 978-1-137-27542-4 PDF
ISBN: 978-1-137-27541-7 Hardback

Library of Congress Cataloging-in-Publication Data is available from the
Library of Congress.

A catalogue record of the book is available from the British Library.

First edition: 2013

www.palgrave.com/pivot

DOI: 10.1057/9781137275424

To Mr. Herbert Pagani, my 10th and 12th grade English teacher, to whom I committed in 12th grade that I would dedicate my fifth book (it was supposed to be my fifth book of poetry, but dramatic criticism will have to do)

And to all of my other influential and inspirational teachers, professors, and mentors, each of whom deserve their own book dedication for how they have helped and shaped me:

Joseph Black, Nicholas Bromell, Jeffrey J. Cohen, Robert Combs, Joseph Donohue, Jill Kasle, Robert McRuer, Mrs. Marcia Pasco (8th grade), Joseph Skerrett, Jenny S. Spencer, and Adam Zucker

Contents

Acknowledgments		vii
	Introduction: Modern Drama and the Translation of History's Narratives	1
1	Danton's Memory: Structural Impossibilities in Büchner's *Danton's Death*	22
2	Salome's Tale—Iokanaan's Telling—Wilde's Retelling: Historical Relativity and (Un)specificity in Wilde's *Salome*	37
3	Galileo's Narrative: Translating History's "Conditions" in Brecht's *Life of Galileo*	58
	Conclusion: For All Seasons—The Particulars and the Universals of Man in Bolt's *A Man for All Seasons*	74
Bibliography		81
Index		88

Acknowledgments

This book was conceived toward the beginning of my graduate studies at the University of Massachusetts, Amherst, and was initiated both by serving as a Teaching Assistant for Joseph Donohue's "Modern American Drama" and writing a paper on *Danton's Death* for Christine Cooper's graduate seminar, "19th Century Discourse and the French Revolution." Therefore, I am truly indebted to both Donohue and Cooper for helping to implant and develop my ideas from their infancy. I would also like to thank readers of this book—J. Chris Westgate, Donald Jellerson, Rebecca S. Hogan, Joseph Hogan, and Jonathon Walter—who provided me with invaluable feedback.

Thanks to Rodopi, Palgrave Macmillan, and the *Journal of Theatre and Drama* for allowing me to reprint parts of Chapter 2 that first appeared elsewhere: Michael Y. Bennett, "A Wilde Performance: Bunburying and 'Bad Faith'" in Michael Y. Bennett (ed.) *Salome and The Importance of Being Earnest*," *Refiguring Oscar Wilde's* Salome, Amsterdam: Rodopi, 2011, 177–179, reproduced with permission of Rodopi; Michael Y. Bennett, *Words, Space and the Audience: The Theatrical Tension between Empiricism and Rationalism* (New York: Palgrave Macmillan, 2012), 54–55, reproduced with permission of Palgrave Macmillan; and Michael Y. Bennett, "Brecht in the Wilde: *Salome's* Liminal Spaces and the Storyteller," *Journal of Theatre and Drama* 7/8 (2001/2002): 145–158, reproduced with permission of the *Journal of Theatre and Drama*.

Also, the section in Chapter 2, *Salome: The Reading*, is reprinted from elsewhere: Copyright © 2004. The Johns Hopkins University Press. This article first appeared in *Theatre Journal* 56.2 (May 2004): 305–306.

palgrave▸pivot

www.palgrave.com/pivot

Introduction: Modern Drama and the Translation of History's Narratives

Abstract: *In order to make sense of the modern "history play," the Introduction presents the three central assertions of this book. First, this Introduction explores the argument that the narration of the past is largely an act of translation. Second, given that the three chapters in this book are concerned with the historical timeframe related to the* telos *(which will be explained in more detail), I argue that we must understand these playwrights acting as "modern" historical translators who fuse the past with the future and, like a translation, say something about their moment in time, bringing past, present, and future together in the tense of* always: *discussing each play's synchronic limitation to a strict time and place (related to its specific historical moment) as well as its diachronic timelessness (speaking to the human condition). And third, modern history plays depart from, especially, early modern history plays in that these modern reincarnations of the form focus not on commemoration (like those in the early modern period) but use history as a means of critique and a way to look at and act in the future.*

Bennett, Y. Michael. *Narrating the Past through Theatre: Four Crucial Texts.* New York: Palgrave Macmillan, 2013. DOI: 10.1057/9781137275424.

> Marcellus (in the Folio and First Quarto of *Hamlet*) or Horatio (in the Second Quarto) asks: "What, has this thing appeared again tonight?" This, I believe, "is *the* question" when beginning to explore different plays and performances about specific historical events. What does it mean to present these events *again* on the stage? What can be seen in *Hamlet* is how a burden (some kind of unfinished business from the past) becomes transformed into an actor's being and doing "this *thing*" on the stage, appearing again in tonight's performance, continuously performing a return of the repressed on the theatrical stage. History can only be perceived as such when it becomes recapitulated, when we create some form of discourse, like the theatre, on the basis of which an organized repetition of the past is constructed, situating the chaotic torrents of the past within an aesthetic frame.
>
> —Freddie Rokem, *Performing History*[1]

Freddie Rokem emphasizes the word "again" in this quotation from his book *Performing History*, which examines how, in performing history on the contemporary stage, the theatre connects the past with the present, "constantly 'quoting' from the past, but erasing the exact traces in order to gain full meaning in the present."[2] Likewise, I would like to return to that word, "again." Actually, Marvin Carlson also begins his book *The Haunted Stage* with the same quote from Shakespeare's *Hamlet*. In responding to this passage through his notions of memory and *haunting*, Carlson quotes Herbert Blau, "*we* [the audience] *are seeing what we saw before*," as well as Bert States: "If something is to be remembered at all, it must be remembered not as what happened but as what happened *again* in a different way and will surely happen again in the future in still another way."[3]

In this book, the question becomes, how is history shown "again" in a modern "history play"? The *Oxford English Dictionary* defines "again" in many ways. The first but now obsolete definition of the word "again" (which has a history of being corrupted with "against") comes closest to its original meaning in Old English, Old German, and Old Norse: "In the opposite direction; back."[4] Shakespeare, according to the *Oxford English Dictionary*, used "again/e" to mean "back into a former position or state; back" and "repetition of an action or fact, once more; any more; anew."[5] It should be noted here that these two Shakespearean uses point, temporally, in opposite directions: the first points "back" and the second, while still pointing to a "former state," has the implication that if the repetition is "anew" the action is done "in a new or different way from the previous."⁶ In the word "again," as in our most common understanding of the word—"repetition of an action or fact"⁷—history plays out "again" (and over and over again) on stage. However, there is an underlying tension present in modern history plays: that between "back" and "anew." This tension between "back" and "anew" in relation to history is both the tension between the *what* of history, what happened ("back"), and the *how*, how history is depicted ("anew"), and also the tension between the *whats*, what constitutes history ("back" or "anew"). Thus, both the problem and the potential for the modern dramatist writing a history play, like a translator, is balancing repetition back to a former state with producing something anew. The dramatist of history and the translator have a narrative that needs translating.

The modern "history play" poses a unique challenge to the traditional tense of modern drama: what my mentor in graduate school, Joseph Donohue, astutely suggests is "drama's *continuing present* that arcs towards an unpredictable future."⁸ Rereading four influential modern history plays that span the timeframe of modern drama (from the "first" modern play to shortly after World War II [WWII])—Georg Büchner's *Danton's Death*, Oscar Wilde's *Salome*, Bertolt Brecht's *Life of Galileo*, and (in the Conclusion) Robert Bolt's *A Man for All Seasons*—this book delves into modern drama's sense and perception of time, and and how its sense and perception of time affects both the present and the future. Ultimately, I argue that the tense of these modern history plays is *always*—in the way that these plays are able to discuss the past, the present, and the future simultaneously—giving the reader a new angle and theory for think about modern drama and theatre's power and methods.

Playing off of, but taking a different angle than Rokem's *Performing History: Theatrical Representations of the Past in Contemporary Theatre* (2000) that juxtaposes the historical past with the theatrical present in order to show how theatre is a witness to the past in the *performance* of contemporary plays, *Narrating the Past through Theatre*, instead, focuses on the *dramatic* tension between the past and the unpredictable future. Chapters 1–3 focus on pre-WWII plays and the Conclusion looks at a play written during the dusk of modern drama. This book suggests that the modern history play is simultaneously an act of narration and an act of translation. However, when transformed into the genre of drama, narration and translation are frequently contradictory but productive endeavors. While "narration" implies a *forward* moving arc, "translation" implies a telling "again", containing both the ideas of "back" and "anew." Thus, while the relationship is complex and contradictory, the merging of the two is a generative affair: producing a piece of theatre that has the ability to comment on (and represent and know, epistemologically) the past, present, and future—creating a unique dramatic tense, the tense of *always*.

In order to make sense of the modern history play, this book has three central assertions. First, I argue that the narration of the past is largely an act of translation. Translation becomes an apt metaphor because playwrights retell a narrative (1) to a different time (and by extension, a different culture), and (2) through different bodies (i.e., the bodies of the actor/character). (And that is not even to mention that I will be reading Büchner and Brecht in translation, which adds another layer, though one not discussed here.) Second, given that the three chapters in this book are concerned with the historical timeframe related to the *telos* (explained in more detail later), I argue that we must understand these playwrights as acting as "modern" historical translators who fuse the past with the future and, like a translation, say something about their moment in time, bringing past, present, and future together in the tense of *always*: discussing each play's synchronic limitation to a strict time and place (related to its specific historical moment) *as well as* its diachronic timelessness (speaking to the human condition). And third, modern history plays depart from, especially, early modern history plays in that these modern reincarnations of the form do not focus on commemoration (as do those of the early modern period) but *use* history as a means of critique and a way to look at and act in the future.

The modern playwright (of historical drama) as translator

Translating the time of the play

As has been noted many times before, the definition of "translate" is "To bear, convey, or remove from one person, place or condition to another."[9] Translation is so often thought of as an act of interpreting a text, not just transferring a story from one language to another, but also displaying the culture of the translator. In this sense, much of translation studies has zeroed in on the "conveyance" from "one person, place...to another." But what about the sense of "condition" in the definition of "translate"? What is the transference of one condition to another condition?

I have previously discussed elements of this issue in relation to Tony Kushner's *Homebody/Kabul*, though not with the exact same intentions that I have here. My central argument about Kushner's play is that Homebody, despite being a (powerful) minoritarian linguist, was still read in translation (thus, no longer in control), which is why she was "dislocated" and "traumatically separated" from her culture.[10] In order to demonstrate that Homebody is a minoritarian linguist, however, I had to show how Homebody—who is British and living in England during the first act (when we actually see the character)—actually comes from a minor culture and speaks a minor language. Given Homebody's use of "forgotten words," I suggest the focus on translation[11] in this play can be, instead, on *time*:

> For Homebody, her language is that of the "guidebook. Its foxed unfingered pages, forgotten words: 'Quizilbash.'" *Homebody is deterritorialized because her words come from another time.* And though the place may be the same physical location (England), it is difficult to argue that late 20th century England is the same *place* as 17th century England, from where words like "gigantine" come. Thus, her native language of forgotten English words is deterritorialized by time and, thus, by place. The language of 17th century England (metaphorically like Kafka's Czech) is subsumed by the dominant language, 20th century English (metaphorically like Kafka's use of German).[12]

Homebody, then, is deterritorialized because her language, and thus (by implication) her culture, is from another time. This goes hand in hand with the idea of translating historical conditions.

Neither Büchner, Brecht, nor Bolt deterritorializes the play through the language in his historical adaptations, but they all translate the conditions of another time (and place) to their current time (and place). We see Büchner's, Brecht's, and Bolt's cultures (and personal selves) through their translations of history's narratives. Wilde's *Salome*, however, offers a special case, as the question posed by Joseph Donohue must be pondered: "What was Wilde doing when he set out to write [the play *Salome*] not only in a tongue but in a form not really his own?" (Donohue, 1994: 86). Wilde, in writing the play *Salomé* first in French and then translating it into English (without the accent), displays that the two texts have many layers of literal and metaphorical translation, as I will discuss in more depth in Chapter 2. While Büchner, Wilde, and Bolt translate narratives in history, Brecht is really the penultimate theatrical translator (to play off of the definition of "translate"); Brecht wants to expose the audience's own culture and "conditions" to themselves by conveying to them, literally and metaphorically, the "conditions" of a previous time/culture.

DOI: 10.1057/9781137275424

One reason for limiting the chapters in this book to modern drama, specifically pre-WWII plays (with a Conclusion that examines a play teetering on the edge of modernity and postmodernity), is that the postmodern notion of multiple truths had not yet been fully established. And, thus, the idea that there existed a historical "chronicle," or that a modern playwright who wrote a modern "history play" was a *theatrical chronicler*, is not so far-fetched. While I am not suggesting that any of the playwrights discussed in this book would have considered themselves theatrical chroniclers, the concept of a "chronicle" that possesses some inherent "transcript" provides a powerful metaphor for translation. Büchner, Wilde, Brecht, and Bolt, thus, translate history's transcript (or history's narrative, if you will) to the language and structure of modern drama, and to another time: "dramatizing the triumph of artistic imagination over mechanical chronologies" through the three analytical foci Brian Richardson suggests are needed in theatre: "story time, text time and stage time."[13] In addition to these strictures, this "transcript" must be grafted onto an actor—an actual body—that *conveys* this historical narrative to another time (i.e., another culture).

While suggestive, it is clear that the modern playwright of historical drama is not quite a theatrical chronicler. What, then, about a *theatrical historian*? Hayden White, in *The Content of the Form: Narrative Discourse and Historical Representation* (1987), discusses both the intersection and the divergence between fiction and history. White's basic thesis is that factual storytelling that takes the form of narrative (i.e., history writing) is related to, if not the function of, the human impulse to moralize reality.[14] The difference between history and fiction is in the content (real events versus imaginary events, respectively) and not in the narrative form.[15] White argues: "The story told in a [historical] narrative is a mimesis of a story lived in some region of historical reality, and insofar as it is an accurate imitation, it is to be considered a truthful account thereof."[16] Along the same lines, the admittedly simple equation that Charlotte M. Canning and Thomas Postlewait relay (to later complicate) in their introduction to their collection *Representing the Past: Essays in Performance Historiography* (2010) is that all historical descriptions are representations.[17] Canning and Postlewait recall Aristotle's notions of narrative in both drama and history:

> Aristotle recognized that history and drama share many mimetic attributes and aims because they represent the possible and probable structures of action ... Both the playwright and historian construct coherent, unified narratives based upon the actions of the agents.[18]

Whereas the playwright may employ the same techniques of narrative as a historian, the historian produces a story of history (a fiction aimed at approximate truth, to echo Michel de Certeau, discussed further later on in this book), while the playwright of history plays uses history to produce stories (to approximate truth, fiction is needed). Therefore, a playwright of history plays is clearly not a theatrical historian.

But can we call this playwright, instead, a *theatrical translator* (of history)? As White reminds the reader on the first page of his book, Barthes argues that narrative is *translatable* without fundamental damage.[19] In the modern sense of the word, "translator" is connected to a person who translates a text from one language to another, whereas in the second half of the sixteenth and first half of the seventeenth centuries (during the emergence of the history play as we most commonly understand it), it was used in the sense of "one who transforms, changes, or alters" and "one who transfers or transports."[20] These two definitions (especially the first) *imply* that a "translator" performs acts upon some *original*, pre-translated thing: as a direct object is needed to be transformed, changed, or altered. Given that there are some or, maybe it is better to say, many historical transcripts available to the playwright of history—whether recorded through oral or written histories or etched in personal or collective memories—the playwright who "transforms" these historical transcripts to the stage is a theatrical translator of history.

Clem Robyns, in a similar vein, argues that translation should not just be considered in the context of "the monolithic and static concepts of 'text,' 'language,' and 'translation.'"[21] Robyns examines the interaction between discourses and discursive structures and strategies to widen the conversation surrounding notions of translation:

> Both the "faithful" translation and the complete transformation of a text or textual element have to be seen as translation strategies. To put it in an extreme way: translation may be anything between literal repetition (which, in practice, does not exist) and intertextuality, in the broadest sense. Secondly, since "cultures" and "literatures" are merely specific types of discursive practice, there is no reason to restrict the concept of translation to the transfer of texts or textual elements between languages (cultures, literatures). So translation can be redefined as "the migration and transformation of discursive elements between different discourses."[22]

Note that the words Robyns uses mirror the sixteenth–seventeenth century definition of translator: "transformation" (twice) and "transfer" ("migration" is not too far off from the idea of "transport"). Therefore, to give Robyns' argument an example (as his essay is theoretical), the playwright who takes a "text" (be it a text, a discourse, a historical transcript, etc.) and transfers it to the stage, transforming this "script" to the discursive structures and strategies of the modern stage, functions as a translator. The narrative of history is transformed into the language of the modern stage: into a language bound by the theatrical realities and structures of (what Richardson says are) "story time, text time and stage time." And, of course, this historical theatrical translator needs bodies, real bodies (of actors), to inhabit, or to be inhabited by, the history's narratives, history's transcripts, and history's *players*.

An argument can be made that historical characters in modern history plays are fictional characters unto themselves (and this is a valid argument), nevertheless an actual body and mind existed and affected real events and people. I discuss in greater detail the complex relationship between remembering and forgetting in chapter 1, where I argue that Büchner chooses drama for this particular plot (as he also wrote fiction) because the actors play out the same mistakes over and over again in subsequent performances. In creating a historical character in modern drama, the playwright needs the reader, the audience, and the actors to *forget* individual and collective *memories*.[23] In other words, Danton cannot know (or the actor must forget, as well as the audience) that Danton is going to die. And this is the point at which the sense of "commemoration" found in early modern history plays that Benjamin Griffin discusses disappears from modern historical adaptations, returning to the medieval "presence" of the Eucharist in a Catholic Mass and the saint plays. An actor playing a historical character in modern drama "abolishe[s] time," like Peter Brown observes about the "*passio*," the medieval narration of a saint's martyrdom: "The hagiographer was recording the moments when the seemingly extinct past and the unimaginably distant future had passed into the present."[24]

Every time an actor takes the stage, especially in a historical adaptation where the outcome is already fixed in time in a particular person(s), both the historical figure(s) and their actions are *present* in the moment of the performance. Elin Diamond says that the past needs fresh actors as the past is *always under construction*.[25] But as Griffin says about the Catholic Mass: "The Mass represents a past event, the sacrifice of Christ; yet that event is understood somehow not to be past, but rather to be perennially repeated through the efficacy of the ritual."[26] The very nature of the theatre (i.e., a fixed dramatic text with new actors playing the same characters in new productions of performances) forces history, through the presence of the actor, to be not quite "under construction" but to be "perennially repeated"—necessarily forgotten in order to be, not remembered, but relearned, or *learned* "again" (both learning *back* and learning *anew*).

The narrative tense of the modern history play

I use the metaphor of a game of cards (which is found in *Danton's Death*, and discussed in the first half of chapter 1) to demonstrate how reading modern history plays through a more traditional tense of modern drama (i.e., a "continuing present") is a problematic endeavor, where the play self-reflexively plays out like a game of cards (i.e., bound by the rules of the game, the cards are reshuffled with different players and slightly different scenarios). Because of the reliance on a fixed dramatic text, history is endlessly bound to repeat itself, even when the *history's players* are different. Danton, whose real life person suffered one death, dies a million deaths on stage, for eternity. While Büchner brings Danton to life, he kills him all the same. This is in stark contrast to what George says in Edward Albee's *Who's Afraid of Virginia Woolf?*: that he loves "the surprise, the multiplexity, the sea-changing rhythm of … history."[27] Through the performance process, the past, both in its limitation to a strict time and place *and* in its timelessness, repeats for its current and its future (not-yet-existent) audiences. And this, most of all, is the progression of modern history plays that we see: from Büchner's realization about both the limitations and possibilities of staging the past to Brecht's notion of an ever-*adapt*able narration of history through Brechtian acting techniques.

Although it is the performance/production of the modern history play that both allows the past to meet the present and gives the past the ability to be translated to future audiences, it is the modern playwright who, when he or she finishes penning a history play, has instantaneously fused the past with the future.[28] For the text (in this specific case, hailing the past) needs the potential of production to consummate itself. Each performance brings the past to the present, but the text inherently contains the possibilities of future stagings. This is where the tense of modern history plays departs with "traditional" plays. The fixing of a "real" past is always in the past because of its location and context in history. Therefore, even when "traditional" plays are set in a fictional past, the tense remains in a "continuing present," with the future always nearby, for in the premise of fiction we suspend our disbeliefs. The audience member watching a modern history play may suspend disbelief that these are not history's "real" players, but the "plot" is "real" (of course, fictionalized or translated rather, to a degree) to the audience.[29] Again, in modern history plays, the production brings the past to the present (as noted earlier in Rokem's *Performing History*); the dramatic text brings the past into the future.

Chris Lorenz, in "Unstuck in Time. Or: The Sudden Presence of the Past" (in the edited collection *Performing the Past*) discusses the history of the academic study of history and the change of "history's temporal framework."[30] Relaying the concept of Francois Hartog's "regime of history," Lorenz explains that before the French Revolution, the "classical regime of history," following Cicero's formulation—*historia magistra vitae*—used history and the past as a "practical *exempla*" for the present; after the French Revolution, with the rise of "'the nation-state' in the making," the "'modern' regime of history" focused on *telos*, where "the future became the point of orientation."[31] It was following WWII that historians focused on a "'presentist' regime of history," where in Hartog's phrasing, "the point of view is explicitly only that of the present,"[32] to which Lorenz adds that presentism "means the presence of a traumatic catastrophe, and 'haunting' past—of a 'past that won't go away,'" which is not based upon *telos*' linear and irreversible conception of time,[33] but where, "in trauma the past stays present (and can return in 'haunting' forms)."[34] Given that this book studies modern drama, the historical timeframe related to the *telos* is most appropriate. In such fashion, these playwrights act as "modern" historical translators, fusing the past and the future. As in a translation, these playwrights also say something about their moment in time. Ultimately, they bring the past, present, and future together in the tense of *always*.

Conceiving the history play

Griffin examines the medieval saint plays and the origins of the history play[35] by tracing their roots from the Eucharist in medieval Catholic Masses to the understanding of the Eucharist in Protestantism. Griffin notes how the sacrifice of Christ in a Catholic Mass is thought to happen again, in the sense that Christ is "present" in the Eucharist and the sacrifice is occurring at the present moment.[36] The spectator of the resacrifice, then, enters "a 'timeless' cultural site," coming into contact with the presence of the dead.[37] With the advent of Protestant prayer books, "the new English service foregrounded the historical contingency of Christ's death," as "the Eucharist *signified* Christ's body and blood."[38] Griffin notes that John Calvin thought that the Roman Mass "wipes out the true and unique death of Christ and drives it from the memory of men."[39] The history of drama, Griffin argues, mirrors this shift in historical sensibility from Catholicism to Protestantism, "creating a new form of historical drama, in which a sense of commemoration takes precedence over the sense of presence."[40] (This sense of commemoration in early modern history plays, as I argue, is something that disappears in modern historical adaptations.)

In early medieval saint plays, "the saints have in some sense traversed or defeated time, as the sacrifice of Christ transformed the nature of time itself."[41] Griffin argues that John Bale's *King Johan* (ca. 1534–1538) was the turning point, which was novel because the universals were readily distinguishable from the particulars.[42] Griffin concludes that Johan is *present* not in reality but in *memory*; unlike the saint play that dramatizes a past conversion, *King Johan* forces the audience to suffer a conversion, with Johan's martyrdom being efficacious only with respect to its future meaning for its Tudor English audience.[43]

In discussing the dialectic between truth and art in history plays (particularly those by Shakespeare), G. K. Hunter disagrees with Samuel Johnson's neoclassical-sounding rule that history plays are "a series of actions with no other than chronological succession," summarizing Johnson's position that history plays are "mere transcripts of history."[44] In discussing chroniclers (particularly Edward Hall), Hunter suggests that such chronicles "exemplify less the grand historical design than the complexity, dispersal, randomness, even incomprehensibility of actual happenings."[45] Even Holinshed's chronicles, Hunter points out, were self-described as a "collection of histories."[46] Therefore, Hunter concludes that a dramatist who reads a historical chronicle "has to achieve his design by means of rigorous exclusion and reshaping."[47]

The genre of the history play (especially Shakespeare's history plays), David Scott Kastan persuasively argues, has less to do with its representation of its subject (i.e., history) and more to do with its dramatic form and the "playwright's sense of the shape of history": the medieval drama had a teleology based upon Creation and Judgment, whereas Shakespeare's plays, while still being linear, do not have a necessary end in sight.[48] However, unlike the Shakespearean history play, which has a linear history (*telos*) with no necessary "end" in sight but that still gives the plays its dramatic form, Silke-Maria Weineck argues that Büchner's *Danton's Death* "does not only revolutionize drama it also contests prevalent models of History"; likewise, Schiller called for (especially in idealist historical drama) coherent, linear order: "Where classical drama constructs integrative order, *Dantons Tod* produces excess."[49] Diamond suggests that in modern/modernity's drama there exists "the anti-humanist, antimimetic bias, the mocking but anxious attitude toward history, the references to fragmentation."[50]

Conceiving the modern history play

The study of the modern dramatization of history necessitates a parallel and interweaving history of history. All history, itself, as Michel de Certeau argues, is a product of the present—"the past is the fiction of the present"[51]—with historical analysis being "next to" present time in how the past is staged, like how a prospectivist produces a future.[52] In this same way, a "beginning" does not explain the present, as each historian envisions a rupture in history where his or her investigation ends: that is, current events determine the past.[53] Thus, historical chronology is composed of "periods" that are constituted when a "decision" has been made to be different or no longer be as such; therefore, each "new" time period has a discourse that considers the "period" preceding it to be "dead," but a past that has already been delineated by former ruptures.[54]

Attilio Favorini and Aleida Assmann present two semi-parallel "histories" both of which are related to drama (and for Assmann, literature as a whole, as well). Favorini, in *Memory in Play* (2008), in discussing the intersection of history and (adding another layer) memory in drama, indirectly addresses the history of creating fictional pasts that reflect the present. Favorini suggests that the "history/memory problem" (i.e., its complex relationship) began at the end of the Middle Ages when the availability of printed texts allowed fact to be more easily distinguished from fiction, leading to what William Nelson has called "the dilemma of the Renaissance storyteller," who had to worry about distinguishing between and constructing two types of stories: fictional and factual.⁵⁵ Most historical plays from the sixteenth to the nineteenth century, Favorini argues, were more concerned with myth-construction, philosophizing, and local politics than the art of memory or research—influenced by the discourse surrounding dramatic conventions of their times.⁵⁶ Shakespeare, too, developed his history plays through a selective memory of English history, driven both by "the master narrative of the Tudor myth" and his own desire to "analogize or critique contemporary *Realpolitik*."⁵⁷ Historical dramas after the Reformation were either romanticized histories, ahistorical, or rewritings of history in order to make, avoid, or reference contemporary politics.⁵⁸ At the end of the eighteenth century, Favorini continues, playwrights no longer remembered history but used it as a pretext, with the past not really being about the past.⁵⁹

It was with nineteenth-century historiography that Favorini sees a crucial rift opening up between history and memory: with industrialization, urbanization, and a rising bourgeoisie, historiographers realized that they needed to construct a "new" past,⁶⁰ with the French Revolution being a watershed moment of theatrical memory of history on European stages.⁶¹ In the twentieth century, the history play was dominated by an ironic stance and a tragicomic mood: embracing anachronism, openly fictionalizing history, and staging "figures of drama" who were not just mere embodiments of historical characters represented on stage but characters that could be intellectually penetrating.⁶²

Another history is presented in Assmann's *Cultural Memory and Western Civilization* (German 1999/English 2011). In the medieval period, according to Assmann, the practice of commemoration was linked to care of the dead and poor and to the institution of purgatory, where (according to Pope Gregory the Great) the fate of the dead could be influenced by the living.⁶³ During the Renaissance, an artist could combat his or her own death by invoking the memory of the dead, pursuing immortality through cultural achievement.⁶⁴ Shakespeare's Histories examine the individual and how memory is unreliable: selective memories make humans limited or biased, but capable of action.⁶⁵ There were five reasons why Elizabethan England had a new version of the past: (1) the monarchy had become a part of the nation-state, signaling a clear schism from the idea of a monarchy as being part of a mythical golden age; (2) there was a need for a new nation to separate itself from memories of the feudal system; (3) the nation and King became the subject of history, being used for and about the nation; (4) plays became educational—providing a history lesson, interpreting history, and monumentalizing history; and

(5) with especially Shakespeare, history helped create a new national myth and national identity.[66] (This echoes Certeau's point that histories are reconstructed ("anew") around moments of schism or to create moments of schism.) The Reformation, then, with its new and binding system of values and it doubt of tradition, created a sharp distinction between the present and the past, a divide that could not be bridged.[67] In the "modern age" (around 1800), compared to earlier eras, the cultural remembrance of the dead faded when the legal rights of a dead person were abolished: effectively erasing not only their legal status but also their social status.[68]

While Assmann clearly demonstrates that William Wordsworth sees memory as a Muse that makes the formation of his personal identity possible as a representative model of the nineteenth-century turn in memory and history,[69] I do not believe that this is how "modern" dramatists engaged with the past. Rather than, as Assmann argues, Romantic memory serving as a replacement (as opposed to a reproduction),[70] starting with Büchner, I argue that playwrights saw the past as something to be *used*. Since the past was a part of our individual as well as collective consciousness, an exploration of the past was an exploration of *us* (both individually and collectively).

Friedrich Nietzsche, in *The Use and Abuse of History* (1874), discusses how history ought to be used. Nietzsche argues that history should be used for life and action (as opposed to being used to avoid life and action, or as an excuse for being selfish, cowardly, or base).[71] Nietzsche sees history's "plastic power" as its greatest strength, suggesting that life needs forgetfulness:

> We must see clearly how great is the "plastic power" of a man or a community or a culture; I mean the power of specifically growing out of one's self, of making the pasts and the strange on body with the near and the present, of healing wounds, replacing what is lost, repairing broken molds.[72]

History must be studied not for the sake of knowledge but "as a means to life."[73] Nietzsche suggests three possible kinds of history, appropriate to different people in different situations: (1) *monumental* history that provides examples, teachers, and comforters to the man of action; (2) *antiquarian* history helps the conservative and reverent person to look back with love and trust to one's origins; and (3) critical history that brings the past to judgment, interrogating and, ultimately, condemning it.[74] Nietzsche concludes with the Greek motto, "Know thyself,"[75] and in this knowing, history is needed only for the service of the future and the present.[76]

"Modern Drama," usually thought of as starting with Henrik Ibsen's *Brand* and *Peer Gynt* (with Büchner being an outlier who anticipated the "modern"), begins at the point when the dramatist observes and accepts "experiences that are lived through," as Ibsen said in 1874 (the same year as Nietzsche's book on the use of history): "But only what has been lived through can be seen in that way and accepted in that way. And the secret of modern literature lies precisely in this matter of experiences that are lived through."[77] Following Nietzsche's suggestion, the past, while not "lived through," is, to the modern dramatist, something that has shaped us and that continues through individual and collective memories to color the way we look and act upon the world. Therefore, it is the job of the modern dramatist to show us our individual and collective memories "again," translated and adapted to their present and future audiences so that these memories can be lived through and experienced "again" (necessary so we see our experiences that we lived through, not blinded by the moment but understood with hindsight). Confronting these memories not only takes us "back" into our individual and collective consciousness but also, importantly, simultaneously makes it "anew," so as to alienate (to use Brecht's idea that will be articulated near the end of "modern drama") the familiar, making the "past and the strange" come into contact with the "near and the present": making us encounter and question our deep-seeded individual and collective assumptions and memories.

Continuing off of Weineck and Diamond's lines of thought, and returning to the idea of commemoration in early modern history plays, I argue that there exists a meta-theatrical self-awareness[78] in these "modern" history plays,[79] if you will, about the very nature of history (i.e., what *happened* and how it relates to capital "H" History, the narrative of history), narration, and translation (and the intersection among the three). Rather than be commemorative as in the early modern period (or also in contemporary society, as Eelco Runia, writing in 2007, argues that the "desire to commemorate is ... the prime historical phenomenon of our time"),[80] modern history plays use history to critique social structures in order to force the audience to make a better world; as Runia says about the post-WWI generation, they "were too busy *making* history to be able to commemorate it."[81] Extending off of Homi Bhabha's assertion that "history may be half-made because it is in the process of being made,"[82] Büchner (writing a generation after the French Revolution and the Napoleonic Wars), Wilde (writing a bit more than a generation after the Great Famine—the Irish Potato Famine—which was a watershed moment in Irish history, leading to increases in nationalism and a diaspora), Brecht (writing a generation after WWI, and observing the rise of fascism), and Bolt (writing a generation after WWII) all looked to history to force their audiences into a state where they must confront the past, the present, and the future, simultaneously: needing to *forget*, not to re-remember, but in order to *learn* "back" and "anew." In other words, by viewing the past, the audience (as Nietzsche more-or-less suggests) must say to themselves: Here are the mistakes of the past that look a lot like the present; so what will we, and what will I, do in the future?

Overview of the book

The chapters that follow provide close readings of the four aforementioned modern history plays. While this book is concerned primarily with modern drama—with literary readings of dramatic texts—issues of performance will not be ignored: each chapter will also discuss specific productions of each play, helping ground my dramatic readings in theatre performance. As mentioned earlier, the three chapters in this book cover the period concerned with the historical conception of the *telos* (post–French Revolution to WWII). The Conclusion, examining Robert Bolt's 1960 *A Man for All Seasons*, offers a space to investigate how the historical study of "presentism" and the notion of "haunting" that came after WWII plays out in a history play that sits on the fence of modern and contemporary drama (modernity and postmodernity).

Chapter 1, "Danton's Memory: Structural Impossibilities in Büchner's Danton's Death," examines how Georg Büchner's *Danton's Death* invokes the workings of history and memory to create a narrative of suffocation, where the desires of narrating the past smash up against the "continuing present (that arcs toward an unpredictable future)" of drama. In effect, *Danton's Death* is a lamentation on *unrealized possibilities* and *lost opportunities*, and the very contradictory nature of dramatizing the past reinforces these almost oxymoronic abstractions. The effectual and ineffectual functions of memory (and it will become the dream for Strindberg many years later) that collapse the past and hopes for the future into a precarious present are exposed only to be forgotten and taken to the grave with the death of Danton. For Büchner, in *Danton's Death*, the failure to remember—that is, the failure of memory and the failure of history to remember—becomes the failure to seize an opportunity; or in another sense, past unrealized hopes for the future become the future's desire for its present.

Chapter 2, "Salome's Tale—Jokanaan's Telling—Wilde's Retelling: Historical Relativity and (Un)specificity in Wilde's *Salome*," discusses the ways in which *Salome sees* and *shows*. In Austin Quigley's words: *Salome* is a play about "the fascination with different ways of seeing." But is it also about different ways of showing and different ways for storytellers to show. I will venture to say that *Salome* exhibits a Brechtian turn in Wilde. Instead of just inviting the audience to consider what they would have done if they were in Salome's position, Wilde seems to ask *himself*: How would I have written this play if I were part of this society? Wilde repositions the storyteller like a Brechtian actor. *Salome*, then, is a *historically relative* adaptation meant to alienate not only the audience but also the writer himself. This chapter, ultimately, discusses Wilde's many translations, some literal and some metaphorical, of *Salome* and how these layers of translation lead to alienation.

Chapter 3, "Galileo's Narrative: Translating History's 'Conditions' in Brecht's *Life of Galileo*," examines Brecht's understanding of the need to convey "conditions" from one time to another, from one culture to another. Focusing on the telescope as the central metaphor and agent of change in the play, I argue that Brecht models the structure of the play after it: creating a *telos*-shaped arc that forces the audience to consider their future actions. Considered in this way, and juxtaposing it with notions of history, I argue that Brecht forces his audience to suffer what Alasdair MacIntyre calls an "epistemological crisis," by pitting historical narratives against one another. The resolution of this created epistemological crisis gets to the very heart of Brecht's notion of what epic theatre attempts to do.

Notes

1. Rokem, *Performing History*, xi.
2. Ibid. xiii.
3. Carlson, *The Haunted Stage*, 1, 3.
4. "Again," *Oxford English Dictionary*, 2nd ed., 1989.
5. Ibid.
6. "Anew," *Oxford English Dictionary*, 2nd ed., 1989.
7. "Again."

8   I am quoting Joseph Donohue's conception of the tense of drama, which he repeated in many "Modern American Drama" lectures at the University of Massachusetts, Amherst.
9   "Translate," *Oxford English Dictionary*, 2nd ed., 1989.
10 Bennett, "Minoritarian Linguist in Translation."
11 In "Performing Translation in Kushner's *Homebody/Kabul*," presented at the University of Massachusetts, April 2004, Jenny S. Spencer noted the absolute centrality of translation to any understanding of Kushner's play. See also Spencer, "Performing Translation in Contemporary Anglo-American Drama," 389–410.
12 Bennett, " Minoritarian Linguist in Translation."
13 Richardson, "'Time Is Out of Joint,'" 308. For an article about contemporary theatre's sense of dramatic time, see Fischer, "Dramatic Time," 241–256.
14 White, *Content of the Form*, 14.
15 Ibid. 27.
16 Ibid.
17 Canning and Postlewait, "Representing the Past," 12.
18 Ibid. 18.
19 White, *Content of the Form*, 1.
20 "Translator," *Oxford English Dictionary*, 2nd ed., 1989.
21 Robyns, "Translation and Discursive Identity," 405.
22 Ibid. 408.
23 Tony Crowley discusses memory and forgetting in relation to Brian Friel's *Translations* and *Making History*. Crowley examines memory and forgetting in a different manner than I do, contemplating the following questions: "Is there an obligation to remember? Is there a duty to commemorate? Does peace depend on forgetting?" (Crowley, "Memory and Forgetting," 73).
24 Qtd. in Griffin, "Birth of the History Play," 221.
25 "The past, Blau asserts, riffing on Marx's *Eighteenth Brumaire*, may or may not replay itself as farce, but it will always need fresh actors—blood donors—because *it is always under construction*. The theatre—and the theatre's literature—is not only a means of transfusion, it is *the means* of transfusion, for what is resuscitated is what had to be invented in the first place" (Diamond, "Modern Drama," 5).
26 Griffin, "Birth of the History Play," 217.
27 Albee, *Who's Afraid of Virginia Woolf?*, 67.
28 G. K. Hunter has an interesting take on how the past meets the future in history plays (particularly history plays by Shakespeare):

> [Shakespeare] seeks to create specific though complex interrelations out of the narrative evasiveness of their "real life" stories, turning parataxis into hypotaxis and in all cases requiring the events to implicate a future that will explain their meaning ... [the history play's] future keeps opening up new possibilities instead of closing them

down: "the king is dead; long live the king." ("Notes on the Genre of the History Play," 237–238)

In another article, Hunter states a similar idea in an interesting fashion:

> History plays are not shaped by the formal closures of death and marriage; they allow the open-endedness of history itself to appear—when one king dies another king emerges; time and politics grind on with a degree of indifference to the life-cycles of individuals. ("Truth and Art," 20)

29 Think of Quentin Tarantino's *Inglorious Bastards* (2009) when many moviegoers had trouble letting go of the fact that Tarantino drastically changed historical events.
30 Lorenz, "Unstuck in Time. Or: The Sudden Presence of the Past," Tilmans et al., *Performing the Past*, 75. For a more philosophical, specifically ontological, approach to history and time, see Bentley, "Past and "Presence," 349–361.
31 Lorenz, "Unstuck in Time," 75.
32 Ibid. 82.
33 Ibid. 83.
34 Ibid. 84.
35 The following, since this book examines the modern history play, is meant only as an overview of the classical conceptions of the history play, which is mostly connected to early modern drama. For more on the subject of the history play, see Shortslef, "Acting as an Epitaph," 11–24; Dillon, "The Early Tudor History Play," 32–57; Ullyot, "Seneca and the Early Elizabethan History Play," 98–124; Kewes, "The Elizabethan History Play," 170–193; Cavanagh, *Language and Politics*, ; Hattaway, "The Shakespearean History Play," 3–24; Hoenselaars, "Shakespeare and the Early Modern History Play," 25–40; Robinson, *Writing the Reformation*; Kurtz, "Rethinking Gender," 267–287.
36 Griffin, "The Birth of the History Play," 217.
37 Ibid.
38 Ibid. 218.
39 Ibid. 220.
40 Ibid. 217.
41 Ibid. 225.
42 "Never before had the 'particulars'—the historical individual characters—been worth treating in terms of their anagogic significance ... the particulars are treated as *derivable from* universals" (ibid. 229).
43 Ibid. 232.
44 Hunter, "Truth and Art in History Plays," 20.
45 Ibid. 18.
46 Ibid. 18.
47 Ibid. 19.
48 "The medieval drama derives its formal stability from its recognition that human time has a fixed beginning and end (the Creation and Judgment).

The shape of the Shakespearean history play, however, is denied this stability because, although time is felt as a linear process as in the Cycles, the ends of this process are nowhere in sight. Individual actions may be brought to completion, but the history play recognizes the impossibility of isolating the action from its place on the temporal continuum" (Kastan, "The Shape of Time," 263, 270).

49 Weineck, "Sex and History," 353. "Though his work is constantly read in terms of his own revolutionary politics, Büchner seems to have been equally interested in writing Rankean history. Perhaps as much as one-sixth of Danton's Tod (1835) was transcribed from the histories Büchner used as sources. His title deliberately evokes the last play of Schiller's trilogy, suggesting that Büchner is both responding to and refuting Schiller's historiography" (Favorini, *Memory at Play*, 67).
50 Diamond, "Modern Drama," 10.
51 de Certeau, *The Writing of History*, 10.
52 Ibid. 8.
53 Ibid. 11.
54 Ibid. 3–4.
55 Favorini, *Memory in Play*, 62.
56 Ibid. 62–63.
57 Ibid. 63.
58 Ibid.
59 Ibid. 64.
60 Ibid. 62.
61 Ibid. 67.
62 Ibid. 69.
63 Assmann, *Cultural Memory*, 24.
64 Ibid. 36.
65 Ibid. 55–56.
66 Ibid. 66–71.
67 Ibid. 42.
68 Ibid. 25.
69 Ibid. 90–92.
70 Ibid. 91.
71 Nietzsche, *Use and Abuse of History*, 3.
72 Ibid. 7.
73 Ibid. 11.
74 Ibid. 12–22.
75 Ibid. 72.
76 Ibid. 22.
77 Ibsen: "Speech to the Norwegian Students," 49.

78 For a similar angle on modern historical drama, see Fischer, "Playwrights Playing with History," 249–265.
79 For three articles on modern history plays (more about specific plays rather than the "genre"), see Crowley, "Memory and Forgetting," 72–83; Hammond, "'Is everything history?'" 1–23; and Carson, "Transformation of History into Drama," 7–21.
80 Runia, "Burying the Dead," 314.
81 Ibid. 321.
82 Bhabha, *Nation and Narration*, 3.

1
Danton's Memory*: Structural Impossibilities in Büchner's *Danton's Death*

> **Abstract:** Chapter 1 examines how Georg Büchner's *Danton's Death* invokes the workings of history and memory to create a narrative of suffocation, where the desires of narrating the past smash up against the "continuing present (that arcs toward an unpredictable future)" of drama. In effect, *Danton's Death* is a lamentation on unrealized possibilities and lost opportunities, and the very contradictory nature of dramatizing the past reinforces these almost oxymoronic abstractions. The effectual and ineffectual functions of memory (and it will become the dream for Strindberg many years later) that collapse the past and hopes for the future into a precarious present are exposed only to be forgotten and taken to the grave with the death of Danton. For Büchner, in *Danton's Death*, *the failure to remember*—that is, the failure of memory and the failure of history to remember—becomes the failure to seize an opportunity; or in another sense, past unrealized hopes for the future become the future's desire for its present.

Bennett, Y. Michael. *Narrating the Past through Theatre: Four Crucial Texts*. New York: Palgrave Macmillan, 2013. DOI: 10.1057/9781137275424.

---

* Earlier versions of this chapter were presented at the Central New York Conference on Language and Literature (2004) and at the International Federation for Theatre Research Conference (2005).

> Nothing was fixed, nothing was settled, nothing was permanent; everything was, as they say in financial circles, to come due this month, or to come due next month. It was a time when kings lasted three months, books an hour, plays half an evening, and constitutions fifteen days. The scene shifted constantly, the nation lived in tents, and as we were part of the nation, we followed the trend.
>
> —Abraham-Joseph Bénard Fleury[1]

> I've heard of a sickness that makes one lose one's memory. Death, they say, is like that. Then, I hope sometimes that death would be ever stronger and make one lose everything. If only that were so! Then I'd run like a Christian to save my enemy—that is, my memory. This place is supposed to be safe. Maybe for my memory, but not for me—the grave would be safer. At least it would make me forget. It would kill my memory here, but back there my memory lives on and kills me.
>
> —Danton, in *Danton's Death*[2]

What Dubravka Knezevic has called "arguably the best historical play ever written," *Danton's Death*, by Georg Büchner, dramatizes the downfall and subsequent execution of Georges Danton during the French Revolution and Terror.[3] Danton was the real-life head of the Committee of Public Safety, and when he later became the president of the Convention, Robespierre took over his old position as the head of the Committee of Public Safety. Once the power over executions was granted to the Committee of Public Safety, Robespierre had Danton executed, effectively eliminating all of his major political rivals. Written in 1835 by the twenty-one-year-old Georg Büchner, the composition of the play situates itself in a precarious position in history and also in the history of drama. Many scholars, now, view Büchner as the first modern dramatist. Though his worked remained largely unknown, and was not produced for quite some time after his death (therefore, his *influence* was very limited), with *Danton's Death*, Büchner's first play, the first "modern" play, was a historical drama. However specific the historicity of the play, in contrast to the clear framework and lines of conflict of melodrama, but more specifically, here, the anticipation of Romanticism by the *Sturm und Drang* writers, Büchner's work signals the blurring of dramatic frame and conflict, creating liminal lines (something not really taken up again until Henrik Ibsen, a bit, but not really seen overtly until the work of August Strindberg and Oscar Wilde's *Salome*). Thus, in a sense, it took a historical work to change the way drama narrativized. Writing in 1835, and very politically active himself, Büchner and his work sat in anticipation of the Industrial Revolution and Marx, and looked back upon the French Revolution.

In this chapter, I examine how Georg Büchner, in *Danton's Death*, narrative of suffocation through the invokcation of history and memory.[4] The desires to narrate finds itself confronting the "continuing present" of drama. *Danton's Death* creates a synchronic and diachronic tense of *always*.[5] Lamenting the *unrealized possibilities* and the *lost opportunities*, Büchner discusses the effectual and ineffectual functions of memory. Memories, Büchner suggests, collapse the past and the hopes for the future into a precarious present. However, memories are also exposed only to be forgotten and taken to Danton's grave. The failure to remember in this play is equivalent to the failure to seize an opportunity.. Initially, Danton's memory and remembrance of history allows him to seize all opportunities. Later, however, Danton still remembers, and his memories are killing him, not because he cannot act on them but because he can no longer convey (or translate, rather) those same messages as effectively as another: Robespierre. Danton and Robespierre remember history very differently. What happens to Danton, in effect, is that, for a short time, Robespierre's translation of history is more favorable to others than Danton's translation of the same events. Danton becomes one of the first theorists of the linguistic turn. Danton realizes that the mistakes of the past cannot save the present, for we only know the past, and therefore the structure of the present, by way of a faulty translation. Action that is taken is based on misinterpretation and, therefore, nothing happens and nothing ever changes. In creating a historical drama that is structurally plagued by impossibility, Büchner sets up a cruel joke of contradictions and "empty noise," and created the ominous path where nobody can escape the *terrors* of a bad translation:

> Actually, the whole affair makes me laugh. There's a feeling of permanence in me which says that tomorrow will be the same as today, and the day after and all the days to come will be alike. It's all a lot of empty noise. They want to scare me. They won't dare.[6]

The fact that Büchner chose drama as the genre of the story is quite telling, as well.[7] Only a few months after the composition of *Danton's Death*,

Büchner dabbled in prose fiction, writing the prose fragment, *Lenz*. His choice of genre, drama, reinforces the plague of memory. Intended to come to life and have a physical and material reality of its own on stage, the realities of the stage dictate that memories necessarily die, and that the actors suffer to repeat the same mistakes over and over again, so that every performance is (essentially) the same as the previous one. Danton is sentenced to eternal death by guillotine, and the knowledge gained by the actors must necessarily be forgotten once the play begins again the next night:

> If there is a hero in this prose drama of the prosaic relations in the fourth year of the French Revolution, then it is the guillotine made sacred by the Jacobins. The guillotine functions simultaneously as metaphor and metonymy. It is a metaphor because in the moment of decapitation the sovereignty of the people is shown in action. It is metonymy because this moment cannot be maintained but constantly demands new moments, new beheadings.[8]

This embodied confusion of tropes plays into a genre that only reifies the ideas that Büchner explores and gives them a similar physical reality. In a play where history hinges on the constant juxtaposition of metonymy and metaphor, humans cannot neatly embody both the trope of metaphor and the trope of metonymy in the body of the actor. The character, then, becomes structurally and logically impossible and is in dire need of a topological translation.

The card game

The insufferable repetition of death and despair thematically opens the play with a game of cards. Flirting with a woman at the card table, by "plott[ing] an affair with the queen," Hérault, a deputy of the National Convention, turns the physical action of a card game into a sexual advance: "The kings and queens fall on top of each other so indecently and the jacks pop up right after."[9] The stacking of the cards, however, not only mirror the physical nature of procreation and birth but also ominously point out the continual "fall" of kings and queens: the indecent, possibly early or treacherous fall of the kings and queens are followed by the rise of more than one jack, vying for power and the throne. This drama, played out with the flick of the cards, only lasts until the cards are reshuffled, and then the same drama can be played over again. The fall of kings and queens is left, somewhat, to chance. However, "it costs money."¹⁰ And to get into this drama, to participate in this rise and fall requires a price: some win and some lose. But there is always a winner, and always a loser. And the cards do not care that previous winners come out losers in the end. The cards have no memory.

Each card player, however, is very aware of the object of the game and remembers each win and loss. As Robespierre says about plotting the fall of Danton, a rival "jack," who in Robespierre's eyes is waiting to pop up and become the "king": "The sin is in our thoughts. Whether thought becomes action, whether the body carries it out—that is pure chance."¹¹ But to Danton, there is even less agency than that, and there is very little that we can do about it: "Time loses us," Danton says. We are merely direct objects. We cannot act, but are acted upon, and therefore, nothing can change:

> It's very boring, always putting on the shirt first and the pants over it and going to bed at night and crawling out again in the morning and always putting one foot before the other—there's no hope that it will ever be any different. It's all very sad...and millions have done it this way and millions will keep doing it—and, above all, we're made up of two parts which do the same thing so that everything happens twice. That's very sad.¹²

When questioned by a fellow deputy of the National Convention, Lacroix, about this resignation and his failure to "cry out against tyranny," Danton replies: "You have a bad memory. You called me a dead saint. You were right...I am a relic and relics are thrown into the street."¹³ As Danton says a moment later: "We haven't made the Revolution; the Revolution has made us."¹⁴ The failure of memory on Lacroix's part was that he forgot that Danton was not an active participant in the Revolution. Saints are made "saints" by the declaration of others; relics are not objects that saints use, but objects that are left behind when a saint dies. Lacroix forgot that *the people* put the dead saint to use with his or her relics, and not the other way around. The system of sainthood, with the martyrdoms, relics, and stories, made the saints; the saints did not make the system of sainthood. Likewise, Danton was made by the Revolution, and thus is not in control of his destiny: "Oh, we are miserable alchemists."¹⁵ We desire to make gold, and we keep on trying, but we just can never seem to do it.

It is only in the minds of an audience that the story will live on. The relics keep the stories of the saints alive and the executioner's stage keeps the stories of the Revolution alive. The Revolution, then, requires a convergence of public and private spheres. What distinguishes the saints, distinguished those that faced the Terror: the public judgment of private lives. Büchner acknowledges this:

> What's the difference if they die under the guillotine or from a fever or from old age? As long as they can walk offstage nimbly and can make pretty gestures and hear the audience clap as they exit. That's very nice—and it's fitting for us. We're always on the stage, even if we're finally stabbed in earnest.[16]

In a uniquely reflexive moment, Büchner shows that there is a public use for private lives, whether it be for entertainment or for instructional purposes, as we see later in the play: "Yes, you got to see people in all kinds of situations. It's good that dying's being made public now."[17]

It is in the vast separation between the public and the private that Büchner deconstructs the idea of knowing, and the utter impossibility of it. In the very beginning of the play, when we witness the card game and the oxymoronic "fleeting exchange" of money and the "rebirth of death," that knowledge and the production of it are fully individual pursuits, in that everything knowable is knowable only through sensory dialectics:

> DANTON: ...we are very lonely.
> JULIE: You know me, Danton.
> DANTON: Yes, whatever "knowing" means. You have dark eyes and curly hair and a nice complexion and you always say to me: dear Georges. But (*He points to her forehead and eyes.*) there—there: what's behind that? No, our senses are coarse. Know each other? We'd have to break open our skulls and pull each other's thoughts out of the brain fibers.[18]

In order to understand, one first must destroy: breaking open the skull renders the brain useless, however; ironically, it is only possible to dissect the brain in that manner. Construction and destruction are intimately joined; gain is only ensured through loss, and one person's gain is another person's loss, just like in the card game.

We observe this same path to knowledge later in the play, the first time that we hear Danton called a relic:

> DANTON: The Revolution is like Saturn, it devours its own children. (*After some thought.*) But they won't dare.
> LACROIX: Danton, you are a dead saint, but the Revolution is not interested in relics. It has thrown the bones of kings out into the street and all the statues out of the churches. Do you think they'd let you stand as a monument?

DANTON: My name! The people!
LACROIX: Your name! You are a moderate, I am one, Camille, Phillippeau, Hérault. For the masses weakness and moderation are the same. They kill the stragglers. The tailors of the red-caps faction will feel all of Roman history in their needles if the Man of September was a moderate to them.
DANTON: Very true, and besides—the people are like children. They have to break everything open to see what's inside.[19]

Reality, portrayals, stories, and history transubstantiate. In the eyes of the public, Danton is a dead saint, a relic, a monument, and a name. He is a different reality in his different public guises. Yet he must be broken open for the public to reconcile his different selves created by the public; Danton is going to feel the wrath of the needles creating his story. The Jacobins are knitting with all of the power of Roman history behind those needles. Through their knitting, the Jacobins will weave Danton into history, eliminating their future concern.

Card games, relics, and the method to gaining knowledge rely on both a required permanence and death that work only through the convergence of the public and the private, and work structurally as oxymoronic impossibilities, in their physical and temporal manifestations. This idea grounds the play; the self-reflexive staged-quality plays out like a reshuffled game of cards with different players and different strategies and slightly different scenarios, but is bound by the rules of either the card game or the rules of the text: the card game functioning as the perfect metaphor for the synchronicity and diachronicity of particulars and the universals. The reliance, then, is on memory to carry forward the past and that which is forever lost to time. But as a historical drama, the translatability of memory and information becomes suspect in a genre that is at odds with the very tense that it understands itself to be in. As Marx opened *The Eighteenth Brumaire of Louis Bonaparte*: "Hegel remarks somewhere that all facts and personages of great importance in world history occur, as it were, twice. He forgot to add: the first time as tragedy, the second as farce."[20] In this vein, *Danton's Death* "falls on top of itself" and then "pops up right after."[21]

The guillotine

The game of cards opens up the play, foreshadowing the events of history, Danton's death, and the play itself; the guillotine is the machine that carries out the foreshadowed death at the end of the play. The guillotine is arguably the most enduring image of the French Revolution and subsequent Terror. While the play ends with Danton being sent to the guillotine, the audience never actually sees him die: that is, the guillotine is never put into action in front of the theatre audience. This is a curious move on Büchner's part, as in the text/dialog, there is a convergence of the public and private in the act of dying: "It's good that dying's been made public now."[22] Büchner realizes that execution by guillotine is a performance, one that performs an action and is done for an audience.[23] If the guillotine literally and symbolically ends the arc of a life, and ends the arc of this play—and after all the play is called *Danton's Death*—the important question is, why does the audience not see Danton's death? As Danton himself proclaims: "I can't die, no, I cannot die."[24]

Philip Smith discusses the symbolism of the guillotine at length, offering this particular machine and the discourse surrounding it as a case study contra Michel Foucault's notion that punishment technology is a material expression of instrumental reason that characterized the machine-like operation, uniformity, and calculability of social control in post-sovereign power punishment discourse.[25] Smith argues—following Émile Durkheim's assertion that punishment has more to do with emotion than routinized power, giving voice to collective outrage at the violation of sacred rules—that the invention of the guillotine was a response to cultural needs: symbolically reflecting the cult of reason, efficiency, novelty, and equality in revolutionary France.[26] As Smith suggests, the guillotine, then, could be coded as enlightened,[27] though detractors, noting the imagery of the headless corpse, argued that the guillotine reified barbarism and monstrosity.[28] Smith concludes with the image of the head as a sign of Gothic imagination, arguing via Mikhail Bakhtin that the executioner's customary holding up of the head to the crowd created a crucial node of semiotic ambivalence around a Rabelaisian body.[29]

Without being allowed to see the guillotine in action in *Danton's Death*, the guillotine cannot be coded as either enlightened or as barbaric/monstrous. The guillotine, itself, is semiotically ambivalent. Or, maybe a better way to say it, is that the absence of a symbol (for the guillotine is quite the symbol of the Terror)—and the symbol of the guillotine metonymically stands in for the Terror—forces the audience to think about the Terror without the use of a mental shorthand. In other words, a symbol like the guillotine reduces the Terror to life circling around a single object, one that is semiotically ambivalent because it is simply an object. It is people who give the guillotine significance, and it is people who put the guillotine to use. Thus, the play must arc towards the guillotine because it is the object through which extreme human actions manifest themselves. But the guillotine cannot be present because the symbol would overtake the human input. Put simply, the focus on the nature of the machine (which, of course, has no nature) would distract the audience from the nature of the people who put the machine to use.

But there is also the question of the public and the private, and its ancillary, the performance of the execution. Part of the terror of the Terror was that the performance of the execution in public turned a crime against the state into a crime against the public. The French Revolution is a significant period because the French went from being subjects of a king to members of a state: the state being an abstract body, an extension of the people. Crime went from more-or-less a crime against the king (and his law) to a crime against the state. The public performance of execution by guillotine took the idea of crime and went one step further. Instead of crime indirectly being against the members of the state, by executing people in public, crime metaphorically became crime against a public made up of individuals. As Robespierre says in an exchange:

> ROBESPIERRE: In the name of the law.
> FIRST CITIZEN: What's the law?
> ROBESPIERRE: The will of the people.[30]

And it was this essentially rhetorical move by the Committee of Public Safety that allowed the Terror to continue in the name of freedom. The crowd at a public execution after the French Revolution was, thus, distracted from seeing themselves as complicit in the execution because crimes metaphorically became crimes against them.

In this respect, Büchner will not let the theatre audience see Danton die. For while Danton's death is a lesson, if you will, in how real people and history "falls on top of itself" and then "pops up right after," the image of a dead Danton would instill an irrevocable finality in the minds of the audience. Büchner would also be implicating the audience as being complicit to allow his death. Instead, while Büchner is pessimistic about human nature, he is not without hope for a better future or for the salvation of humanity. Büchner does not want to stain the audience, allowing them the ability to do something about their present and their future. While Danton has to die (because of history and History), Büchner saves Danton from the act of dying in a sort of *deus ex machina*.

Although Büchner cannot save Danton from history, Büchner can save history from repeating itself for the pure sake of performance, much like how the guillotine was used in public for the sake of performance. While Danton does die over and over again every time the play is performed, Büchner's sympathy towards Danton—by taking his dying out of his death—removes the terror from the Terror. It is not that Büchner wants the Terror to be less terrifying, but the visceral reaction to the guillotine invokes a displaced terror: terror at the object rather than the terror of human action.

Danton's Death in production

Robert Wilson and the audience member as interpreters of history

Andrzej Wirth, in a review of Robert Wilson's famous and controversial production of *Danton's Death* at the Abbey Theatre in Houston in 1992, discusses the centrality of the guillotine in Wilson's production:

> Wilson's abstracting attitude has a cooling effect, and the universal bloodletting of the story, compared in the text to the rituals of the Stone Age, is set by Wilson in the Age of Ice. The guillotine in the last scene is reduced to such a perfect cubistic stage object, that the execution of Danton is perceived more as an aesthetic closure than as a tragic historical event...the real protagonist of the evening is the thrust stage itself, poetically transformed by Wilson into a form resembling a giant guillotine, that kills with the sharpness and speed of light. Its blade falls down...or closes vertically...with the finality of closure unattainable through verbal expression alone.[31]

The guillotine is not just a symbol in Wilson's production it is also a part of the narrative structure of the play: even the thrust stage—the space of the play—"kills with the sharpness and speed of light."

Ellen Halperin-Royer spent time at the Abbey Theatre, where she was able to sit in and watch a three-week workshop and a six-week rehearsal period of Robert Wilson's production.[32]

> Wilson stated that he hates naturalism, that to act naturally onstage is a lie. Wilson explained his preference for a formal, more distant theatre in which the audience can enter at will and actively interpret the images onstage. Far from telling the audience what to think or feel, Wilson wants to ask provocative questions for each audience member to answer individually.[33]

DOI: 10.1057/9781137275424

What was Wilson having the audience members interpret? Katherine E. Kelly, in her review of the same production in *Theatre Journal*, suggests that Wilson was creating a "painting of history":

> In a letter of apology addressed to his parents, Georg Büchner defended his controversial rendering of the French Revolution by aligning himself with history: "I was compelled... to show the men of the Revolution as they were; bloodthirsty, dissolute, vigorous, and cynical. I regard my play as an historical painting, which must be like its original." Robert Wilson's adaptation of Büchner's plaay is a sort of literally three-dimensional painting of history in his minimalist signature, visually abstracted but bursting with intertextual references to prior works of art.[34]

Kelly concludes:

> In Wilson, the painting is the message. As always, he privileges the spectator's "freedom" and "choice" in his pacing and scale. But my guess is that the answer to questions about Wilson's politics and intentions lies buried inside his consciousness of earlier productions he's seen of this play—what he called "noisy" productions. Wilson looks for where he can make a difference. This was to be a quiet *Danton's Death*.[35]

The audience member at Wilson's production was forced to interpret history just like Robespierre and Danton. The only difference was that the audience member's interpretations did not (necessarily) have the same outlet and the same platform that Robespierre and Danton had during the French Revolution. Both Robespierre and Danton first needed to interpret history in order to translate it to the masses (much like the scholarly reviewers, each of whom translate the same "event" to their audience in a different manner). This puts the audience member in an unusual position. It became possible (though I was not there, but by extending the arguments presented in the reviews) to understand not only the necessity associated with interpreting history, or a "painting of history," but (maybe if Wilson got through to the audience member) also the responsibility of wielding such "freedom" and "choice.

While Wilson is not a Brechtian director, as the above readings of his production of *Danton's Death* attest, this play and Wilson's "quiet" (possibly contemplative, might be a good word) production supports a reading of the play by Jutka Devenyi. Devenyi argues that Büchner by juxtaposing the public and private scenes, created by a schism between scenes that take place in Danton's world and in the streets of Paris, represents Danton's distance from the realities of his time.[36] By oscillating between

Danton's mind and the streets of Paris in this synecdochic structure, Büchner produces a certain alienation effect because the audience must construct the context of the fragmented episodes, thereby never being allowed enough time to completely empathize with Danton: the audience, then, remains psychologically distant.[37]

The French Revolution: pretext or subject?

This Brechtian reading of the play returns us to the question of history and how Büchner was engaging with history. I think, though, the question as to what Büchner's play is about still lingers. Is Büchner actually writing *about* the French Revolution? Or is the French Revolution merely used as a *pretext* in order to discuss the human story of Georges Danton? Or something else? I am not trying to dismiss the entire body of the play by focusing only on the beginning and the end. However, I think, while the majority of the play gives the audience the plot and the story of Danton and the French Revolution, it is possible for Büchner to be self-reflexive through beginning the play with the card game and ending the play with the absence of the guillotine being put to use. And while I discussed the self-reflexive nature of these two parts of the play above, I need to focus on each again in order to examine what *Danton's Death* is actually about.

In a card game, as discussed before, each time the cards are shuffled, different players play out different hands. However, all hands are bound by the rules of the game. Apart from issues of performance and even history (both examined above), the idea of a card game needs to be teased out even further. Each deck of cards contains a finite number of cards and a finite number of specific cards. And the rules of a card game determine each card's *value* and *use*. So while every game of cards will have the same rules, and the cards will have the same value and use, there are multiple types of card games. And therefore, the value and use of each specific card is not fixed. For example, in one type of card game, an ace might be the most valuable card (or most useful) whereas in another it might be a liability. So although a deck of cards may appear to have an independent, logical set of values, this could not be further from the truth. In basic mathematics, the integral numbers 2–10 have a constant value. Humans *use* mathematics and these numbers (which, although they are human constructs are supposedly universal, more-or-less logical concepts independent of subjectivity). In a game of cards, on the other hand, the cards are subject to human will and, maybe more importantly, human desire. And it is this human element that destabilizes the value and use of things (i.e., in this case the specific cards)—things that appear to be logical concepts or objects independent of human input—and turns them into things that manifest themselves to us only through subjectivity.

Regardless of whether we can say that the play is about the French Revolution or it is used as a pretext, we can see the French Revolution serving as the point where the rules that were chosen and made through one central place (i.e., the voice and body of the king) transforming to players sitting around the card table (typically, either each player sitting in a circle where there is no head, or in a regular polygonal table where every player sits at the head of the table), where the rules can be changed by any of the players, though usually by the victor. While people usually take turns being a dealer within each game, when someone wins the entire game playing someone else's rules (i.e., with the game usually decided by the previous winner), then that person usually gets to decide what the new game will be, with its own set of new rules.

Similarly, in history, there appears to be a logical chronology of events that happened in one particular manner. But history is just like a game of cards: the winner of the previous game gets to choose the game. Therefore, the winner gets to choose the rules, with its corresponding values and uses. This is how *history is lived through*, and also how we *live through history*. The dealings of Danton and Robespierre in this play show how humans both create history and are created by history. But, ultimately, *Danton's Death* is about the very nature of telling stories: the nature of chronology, narrative, and arc and how linguists such as Danton and Robespierre translate these events into stories for an audience. *Danton's Death* contemplates the truth behind fiction and the fiction behind truth. This finally brings us back to the guillotine. While Büchner cannot change the events of history, he can set the game he wants to play.

Notes

1   Abraham-Joseph Bénard Fleury, *Memoirs*, 2:398, quoted and trans. in Carlson, *Theatre of the French Revolution*, 244. Fleury was a French actor of the Comédie-Française before, during, and after the French Revolution. He was imprisoned for a time as an antirevolutionary.

2 Büchner, *Danton's Death*, 64.
3 Knezevic, "Marked with Red Ink," 407.
4 Attilio Favorini offers a clear etymology of "history" and "memory" in his article "History, Collective Memory, and Aeschylus," 99–111. He writes:

> *Mnema* and its cognates are associated with the faculty of memory and memorial objects, while *historia* is sometimes used as a synonym with *logos* or narrative, and a historian is called a *suggrapheus* (one who writes down facts), a *logographos*, or a *logopoios*, as well as a *historikos*. *Mnemonsyne* or memory, or course, is the mother of the Muses because before the invention of writing, memory was the poet's chief gift. That Clio the Muse of history is one of memory's offspring offers a mythological foundation for the generation of history out of memory. (99)

5 I am quoting Joseph Donohue's conception of the tense of drama, which he repeated in many "Modern American Drama" lectures at the University of Massachusetts, Amherst.
6 Büchner, *Danton's Death*, 64.
7 See Rokem, "Narratives of Armed Conflict," 555–573. Aptly explaining how "history has become the tragedy itself," Rokem describes repetition in both history and theatre by commenting on Fortinbras' command, "Go bid the soldiers shoot," in *Hamlet*: "The 'agains' of history, with the events from which it constituted—the command to shoot that is apparently repeated in every generation—have merged with the ghosts of tragedy that will in various ways appear on the stage tonight" (559).
8 Müller, "Identity, Paradox, Difference," 525–526.
9 Büchner, *Danton's Death*, 28.
10 Ibid. 28.
11 Ibid. 51.
12 Ibid. 54.
13 Ibid. 54–55.
14 Ibid. 55.
15 Ibid. 55.
16 Ibid. 56.
17 Ibid. 108.
18 Ibid. 27.
19 Ibid. 46–47.
20 Marx, *Eighteenth Brumaire*, 15.
21 Büchner, *Danton's Death*, 28.
22 Ibid. 108.
23 This idea, of course, comes from the idea that there is a "consciousness of doubleness" in performance, according to Richard Bauman, and quoted and explained in detail by Marvin Carlson: see Carlson, *Performance*, 6.

24 Büchner, *Danton's Death*, 91.
25 Smith, "Narrating the Guillotine," 27–29.
26 Ibid. 29–31. "In a sequence of path-breaking, passion-filled debates in May and June 1791 it was decided, against fierce opposition, to retain the death penalty, but in a form compatible with the new spirit of the age. While the ancient régime had allowed class distinctions to be demonstrated in the application of death (nobles were beheaded with a sword, commoners hung), under the new laws each person would die in exactly the same, egalitarian way" (ibid. 32).
27 Ibid. 33–34.
28 Ibid. 37–40.
29 Ibid. 45–46.
30 Büchner, *Danton's Death*, 35.
31 Wirth, "Thrust Stage as Guillotine," 60–61.
32 Halperin-Royer, "Robert Wilson and the Actor," 320.
33 Ibid. 328.
34 Kelly, Review of *Danton's Death*, 375.
35 Ibid. 377.
36 Devenyi, "Consciousness and Structure," 43.
37 Ibid.

2
Salome's Tale—Iokanaan's Telling—Wilde's Retelling: Historical Relativity and (Un)specificity in Wilde's *Salome*

Abstract: *Chapter 2 discusses the ways in which* Salome *sees and shows. I venture to say that* Salome *exhibits a Brechtian turn in Wilde. Instead of just inviting the audience to consider what they would have done if they were in Salome's position, Wilde seems to ask himself: How would I have written this play if I were part of this society? Wilde repositions the storyteller like a Brechtian actor.* Salome, *then, is a* historically relative *adaptation meant to alienate not only the audience but also the writer himself. This chapter, ultimately, discusses Wilde's many translations, some literal and some metaphorical, of* Salome *and how these layers of translation lead to alienation.*

Bennett, Y. Michael. *Narrating the Past through Theatre: Four Crucial Texts.* New York: Palgrave Macmillan, 2013. DOI: 10.1057/9781137275424.

Norbert Kohl describes the characters in Oscar Wilde's *Salome* as "puppet-like."[1] This is a shorthand description, one that Kohl never really explicates before or after the characterization. It appears to be a simple adjective for Kohl to emphasize the somewhat flat nature of the characters in *Salome*, each of whom have "their one fixation."[2] This description, however, is too suggestive to be ignored. What happens to Wilde's *Salome* if we see its characters as "puppet-like"?

Puppetry allows for a production where the strings are visible. In effect, the entire production becomes quite visible to the audience. By separating the actor from the character, a liminal space, represented by the string, is created. This space is one of unexpected possibility for all involved—the actor, the character, and the audience. This element of puppetry allows us to "conceive of the actor as the *producer* of the signs that communicate a dramatic character, rather than as, necessarily, the producer *and* the *site* of those signs."[3] Thus puppetry exposes the spaces in-between the actor and the character, in-between the audience and the character, *and* in-between the audience and the actor. This opens up a bigger space between the playwright and his or her play, its actors, and its audience. And somewhere within all of these tangible spaces the meaning is transmitted to the audience.

Bertolt Brecht, as I will explore in chapter 3, wanted to see the strings; he wanted the audience to be aware that they were watching a play, and with this understanding to become somewhat alienated from the story. According to Austin Quigley, as quoted earlier in this book, *Salome* is a play about "the fascination with different ways of seeing."[4] But, I argue that it is about *showing*, as well. As quoted in the Introduction, "The question must be asked, what was Wilde doing when he set out to write [the play *Salome*] not only in a tongue but in a form not really his own?"[5] Taking a slightly different approach than Joseph Donohue, by discussing different ways that storytellers show, I argue that *Salome* anticipates some of Brecht's notions of the theatre. Not just asking the audience, what would you do if you were in Salome's position, Wilde seems to ask *himself* how he would write this play if he were a part of Salome's society. In *Salome*, the storyteller is repositioned like a Brechtian actor.

While the Salome/St. John the Baptist tale is biblical, appearing in two of the Gospels, it is also historical, appearing in Flavius Josephus' *Antiquities of the Jews*. Wilde's *Salome*, then, is a *historically relative* modern history play meant to alienate not only the audience but also the writer himself. This alienation is due to Wilde's multiple translations: Wilde imbues

Salome with a nineteenth-century self-transplanted Irishman's translation of another time and place. Wilde, then, as Ian Andrew MacDonald shows in minute detail, translates his French text into biblical English. The overall effect of these multiple translations is an almost-fantastic retelling of the beheading of St. John the Baptist: only this version of the story says more about Wilde and nineteenth-century notions of the past and the present and how Wilde wants the audience to be alienated in order to think about their future than it says about biblical Judea.

Salome: the character

Who is Salome? She is a contradiction, a true question and a true answer. She is the "moon": that which is looked upon for light, yet she brings darkness in death (to The Young Syrian and the prophet Iokanaan). This "beautiful" princess who "is like the shadow of a white rose in a mirror of silver" is indeed a shadow.[6] For it is hard to see her for what she is, but we can see her movements, and we can see how those movements push the play along. She is "naked" in that sense.[7] Her movement will not be clothed. Though her motivations are numerous (Herod killed her father and covets her, and her mother's intentions are just as questionable), her love and malice toward Iokanaan is questionable; it is clothed and shadowy: "Through the clouds of muslin she is smiling like a little princess."[8] She is always "like" something; she is an approximation, a simile, a representation, a likeness, but she never *is* something. Salome is like (or maybe is) a *penumbra*: "The partially shaded region around the shadow of an opaque body, where only a part of the light from the luminous body is cut off; the partial shadow, as distinguished from the total shadow or *umbra*; *esp.* that surrounding the total shadow of the moon."[9] She makes it difficult to see where the true shadow ends and the light begins. Somewhere in-between Herod and Iokanaan she moves. She is both seer and murderer, but in fact she is neither. (In addition, she oscillates somewhere in-between the spaces of classic Greek drama and modern drama, somewhere between the fate of the cruel gods and the tortured individual, yet she belongs to neither group.) And finally, she is also the presence in the absence, for Herod seeks her in the eaten parts of fruit: "I love to see in a fruit the mark of thy little teeth."[10]

What are the spaces between which she moves? Salome moves between two main worlds: the world of the servants and the world of the servers.

She moves in and out of Herod's court and in and out of the soldiers' wing. Although belonging to neither, she occupies both spaces. Salome is also constantly present in the thoughts of Herod or the soldiers when she is gone, but she becomes troublesome and worrisome to them when she is present. She fills the halls in-between, but is really the movement in-between the ruler and those ruled. Salome connects by way of disconnecting. She is present only in the teeth marks that she leaves behind. Therefore, she is doubly hard to grasp; she is a mirror image of a shadow (she "is like the shadow of a white rose in a mirror of silver"). She is only a representation of darkness. In effect, those that look upon her are the real shadows; they are the dark figures in the play.

Salome is a play about movement that, in its search, seeks out sexuality, but finds unexpected sexuality and death. The movement associated with Salome's own death is particularly important. We can see from the Rosenbach *Salome* that Oscar Wilde clearly thought about the placement of the staircase. In his own hand, Wilde crossed out, in pencil, the staircase that he placed upstage left and, again in pencil, placed it downstage right.[11] Though it is not possible to know for certain, one can surmise that by moving the staircase closer to the audience, Wilde wanted to make it even more prominent.

The unused staircase looms throughout the entire play. The staircase's prominence is unmistakable, and there is a tension that has built up around it since it has not been used. The audience must wonder who is going to enter or who is going to leave by way of the staircase. It is not until the final moments of the play that this question is answered. After Herod hears that Herodias is pleased by Salome's request for the head of Iokanaan, Herod ascends the stairs. The stage directions read:

> The slaves put out the torches. The stars disappear. A great cloud crosses the moon and conceals it completely. The stage becomes quite dark. The Tetrarch begins to climb the staircase.[12]

In this darkness—where the moon that has so often been likened to Salome is concealed by "a great cloud"—the audience sees the realization of Salome's perverse dreams, her liminal desires: she has kissed the lips of Iokanaan. Herod is halfway up the staircase when he observes this and it is from that position that he subsequently sentences Salome to death. But even in death, Salome cannot be named and pinned down. The approximation of her, not Salome, is sentenced to death: Herod says: "Kill that woman!"[13] Salome is crushed beneath the shields of the soldiers, and when the play ends, Herod still remains halfway up the staircase. Herod stands far above Salome's body, his authority is evident, but he is left somewhere in the middle of the stairs, somewhere between the bottom and the top:

> Exits, too, are important moments in the performance for, apart from their role in structuring the performance continuum, they function very powerfully to activate the offstage as fictional place... The actor is the active agent whose physical comings and goings make manifest the interface and the exit is a particularly potent moment in raising the spectators' consciousness of the "there" beyond the "here."[14]

Thus Salome's "exit" and Herod's exit help confuse the world and space of the play: Salome's presumed death is hidden from the audience by the shields, and Herod never quite exits.

Salome's first lines in the play reveal the impossible predicament of *being Salome:* "I will not stay. I cannot stay. Why does the Tetrarch look at me all the while with his mole's eye under his shaking eyelids?"[15] Presumably, the third line, which discusses Herod's gaze upon Salome, explains the fact why Salome "will not" and "cannot stay." The idea of her staying or leaving because of a gaze raises four points. (1) Implied in the idea of *stay*—"To cease moving, halt"[16]—is the idea that staying is a temporary state. "Moving" is the activity that is stopped. For Salome, then, her home—the palace—is a place where *she* ceased moving (*she* "cannot stay"); the palace, itself, is also a temporary home. In a metaphoric sense, Salome does not belong in the palace. The palace is a holding ground both for herself and for her movement. In this sense, staying in the palace is a liminal act for a liminal character, stuck in an in-between. However, outside of the palace, in scenes with The Young Syrian, we recognize that Salome does not belong there either, as nobody is her equal. (2) If Salome leaves the palace, then, Salome will no longer live in a place designed to house a princess. Her very stay at the palace implies her royalty. However, the temporariness of the stay suggests that it is possible that once she leaves the palace, an element of her royalty will leave her as well (as her departure would imply a disownership of the King and Queen). (3) Whether or she stays or leaves, Salome's identity is couched in her location: in either place, a part of Salome does not exist (whether her ability to move or her birthright as a princess). (4) The "gaze" of Herod turns Salome into a commoner: as the *object* of his gaze, Salome becomes his *subject*. This is a paradoxical, liminal state for Salome. What all four of these points have in common is that Salome is a paradox. Salome has no ability *to be Salome*. The impossibility of *being Salome* highlights the fact as to why Salome is always described "like" something. Just like Salome's "stay" in the palace denotes her temporary state, *being like* something, instead of *being* something displays the inexactitude of *being Salome*.

However, there is one instance when Salome is defined with certainty: Salome introduces herself to Iokanaan, "I am Salome, daughter of Herodias, Princess of Judea."[17] (Note the fact that Herod has nothing to do with her identity in this pronouncement.) The significance of this introduction lies in the fact that Iokanaan is the prophet, who metaphorically sees all but does not know her to be Salome until she states it herself. Metaphorically, it is the prophet who sees, but in this case he is blind to her identity. Thus, Salome only feels comfortable with who she is (as she states it above with exactitude) when a person (in this case, Iokanaan) does not see or gaze upon her *as Salome*. Salome, then, is in an awful predicament.

She is only herself, Salome (to herself in "earnest"), when she is *not Salome* to others. Likewise, as long as she remains "Salome" to others, she simultaneously is *not Salome in earnest*. Salome's change of location, both inside and outside of the palace, is Salome's version of bunburying. Like Algernon and Jack in *The Importance of Being Earnest*, Salome is in a constant state of simultaneously "being" and "not being" while her location changes. In both instances, Salome remains the object of the gaze. However, outside the palace, The Young Syrian is gazing, metaphorically, up at her, just as he gazes up at the moon, the object that Salome is "like." Similarly, inside the palace, Herod gazes down at Salome as his subject. Confusion as to Salome's place abounds when she is inside. Salome both is commanded by Herod to dance, and commands Herod to give her the head of Iokanaan. Likewise, Salome is addressed by Herod as "Salome" when asked to dance for the last time, "Dance, Salome, dance for me,"[18] but when Herod looks back down at Salome at the end of the play from midway up the stairs, he says, "Kill that woman!"[19] No matter her location, for Salome, it is just as difficult "to be" as "not to be."

When Herod calls her "that woman" (as opposed to "Salome"), there is a parallel to when Iokanaan does not recognize Salome, for Wilde suggests through the stage directions that Salome is, in fact, herself at this precarious moment. In the stage directions, Wilde writes that the soldiers kill "*Salome, daughter of Herodias, Princess of Judea.*"[20] This references back to Salome's own pronouncement of who she is when she first meets Iokanaan. It is in her moment of death, when Herod no longer sees her as "Salome," that Wilde suggests that Salome is, again, herself and free of

Herod in terms of her identity. And thus, it is impossible *to be Salome:* for only in death is Salome herself, as suggested by Wilde's stage directions.

Iokanaan: the storyteller

Salome is a remarkable character, certainly, in Wilde's portrayal. It is hard to imagine many audience members, after seeing Salome kiss Iokanaan's lips while his bloody head rests on a platter, saying: "that's how I would act." Wilde not only adapts a biblically historical event, but he also names the play *Salome* after the character most easily defined by his or her contradictions and liminality in the St. John the Baptist story. But Salome's liminality and the subsequent ease of portraying Salome by a Brechtian actor addresses only one of the reasons why Wilde's *Salome* anticipates Brecht's notion of theatre. For the other reason, we must turn to the storyteller: Iokanaan.

It is the storyteller who overtly shows. And in this play, Iokanaan is the active and the detached storyteller. Much of the dramatic plot is told through him. Through his Greek-like riddles and his prophesies (and in language just as imprisoning as Salome's language[21]), the audience learns how Herod ascended the throne and hears how his descent will occur. In this sense, Iokanaan is, to some extent, detached as a storyteller. But Iokanaan actively precipitates the action with these stories, for Salome is Iokanaan's audience, and to enjoy him, to fall in love with him, she kills him. In other words, in *Salome*, Wilde suggests that the storyteller, in order to be loved by the audience, must die or be removed from the space of the story. But at the same time, Wilde is inextricably present in the text. For the language of the play, in its grandiloquence, cannot be the language of characters, but of a playwright/storyteller adapting the story of these characters.

To demonstrate Wilde's connection to the language he uses, Joseph Donohue notes Yeats' reaction to meeting Oscar Wilde for the first time:

> "My first meeting with Oscar Wilde was an astonishment," Yeats recalled in his autobiography; "I never before heard a man talking with perfect sentences, as if he had written them all over night with labour and yet all spontaneous." Readers of Wilde's writings, and audiences of his plays, have often had this same paradoxical impression of evident craft and spontaneity. For generations, those same readers and audiences have consistently associated the man with the writings and the writings with the man.[22]

In writing *Salome*, in writing "a play not only in a tongue but in a form not really his own," Wilde makes his audience see his own alienation (the necessary alienation of the storyteller), which positions him to be able to further alienate his audience). By creating puppet-like characters with alienating language and an alienated storyteller, both present and absent in the play, Wilde has exposed all of the strings of the play and has, therefore, begun to anticipate Brecht's notion of theatre.

I would like to examine the Grandmother's tale in Georg Büchner's *Woyzeck* as a "tale" and use it as a working parallel. The Grandmother's tale and *Salome* are productive comparisons because of the ways in which they are both similar and dissimilar.

These are tales of movement. But these two tales differ tremendously in their historical specificity. *Salome* demonstrates that which is "historically relative," to use Brecht's term, whereas the Grandmother's tale is *historically unspecific*. This is Brecht's explanation of why historically relative plays are particularly valuable for the modern audience:

> If we ensure that our characters on the stage are moved by social impulses and that these differ according to the period, then we make it harder for our spectator to identify himself with them. He cannot simply feel: that's how I would act, but at most can say: if I had lived under those circumstances. And if the play works dealing with our own time as though they were historical, then perhaps the circumsta nces under which he himself acts will strike him as equally odd; and this is where the critical attitude begins.[23]

Although Brecht's analysis here is considered somewhat revolutionary to the theatre, Oscar Wilde himself had recorded these basic sentiments in a letter to the actress Mary Anderson, more than 70 years earlier: "the essence of art is to produce the modern idea under the antique form."[24] Later, Wilde adds:

> An audience longs to be first out of sympathy, and ultimately in sympathy, with a character they have loved: they desire it; they demand it; without it they are not contented; but *this sympathy must not be merely emotional, it must have its intellectual basis*.[25]

Whereas the historical specificity of *Salome* and the court of biblical kings alienates the audience and makes them ask the question, "What if I had been Salome?", the Grandmother's tale alienates not just the boy but also the audience: "A representation that alienates is one which allows us to recognize its subject, but at the same time makes it seem unfamiliar."[26]

The overt historical unspecificity makes the short tale historically relative, in that the tale is definitely not taking place now. In this sense, both these instances demonstrate Brecht's A-effect.

Although I am focusing on ways in which Brecht's notion of theatre was anticipated in both these tales, I am not being totally fair to the genre. It is problematic to pin down both the Grandmother's tale and *Salome* in this regard: they are liminal tales in liminal genres. If it were desirable (and we can ask why it would or would not be at a different time) to classify these two tales as representative of a certain genre, we might run into many problems. How do these function as myths? Are they fairy tales even though they do not have happy endings? Are they, rather, folk tales? I do not really want to go into the particularities of different categories of folk tales as this is not the goal of this inquiry, and much good scholarship has already been done on the subject,[27] but it is important to consider how the Grandmother's tale and *Salome* work like myths, fairy tales, parables, and so forth. More importantly, in relation to this particular study, we need to examine how these tales function politically.

As Kohl notes, Wilde proclaimed the autonomy of art, but he had difficulty in conforming to these principles in his fairy tales. Kohl goes on to demonstrate how Wilde was aware of this problem by recalling the end of "The Devoted Friend": "the linnet confesses to having told a 'story with a moral,' to which the duck replies: '... that is always a very dangerous thing to do'—an observation confirmed by the authorial narrator: 'And I quite agree with her.'"[28] What is dangerous about stories with morals? Or more importantly, we might ask, who is in danger?

Jack Zipes, in his book *Fairy Tale as Myth: Myth as Fairy Tale*, might rephrase the question to ask who benefits from stories with morals. In his lucid introduction, Zipes carefully argues that for fairy tales and myths, the "ideological impact is great"[29] for "[maintaining] the hegemonic interests of the bourgeoisie."[30] In copying particular tales, hegemony is reinscribed: "To copy a fairy tale is to duplicate its message and images, to produce a look-alike. To duplicate a *classical* fairy tale is to reproduce a set pattern of ideas and images that reinforce a traditional way of seeing, believing, and behaving."[31] But *Salome*, as Quigley argues, is about different ways of seeing; Salome's kiss, and Wilde's bloody portrayal of it, demonstrates different ways of behaving; and finally, ultimately, as I suggest, *Salome* is about different ways of showing. And if we think about it in this way, maybe we could consider *Salome* (and possibly the Grandmother's tale in Büchner's *Woyzeck*) as *showing* subversive storytellers. Traditionally, "the emphasis in most folk tales was on communal harmony. A narrator or narrators told tales to bring members of a group or tribe closer together."[32] However, in *Salome* and in the Grandmother's tale we encounter narrators—Iokanaan and the Grandmother, respectively—whose narrations do anything but bring members of a community closer together. We are looking not at revisions that "[correspond] to changed demands and tastes of audiences,"[33] but instead these are wild (or Wilde) adaptations of traditional forms: Iokanaan subverts local history, and the Grandmother does the same with a seemingly simple fairy tale. These adaptations (again, of traditional narrational forms) are wholly alienating, and Brecht made adaptation a common practice in his theatre.

I think the one element that we do not want to forget here is that there are storytellers who tell these tales. What are the motivations of the storytellers? Why do Iokanaan and the Grandmother tell their tales? With any tale, this question cannot be ignored. As long as there is a storyteller, there is some motivation for telling the story. Whether fairy tales are told to reinscribe the ideologies of the dominant culture or to subvert them (as in the case of *Salome* or the Grandmother's tale), there is an agenda (even in entertainment): *everything is political.*

But Iokanaan is not a simple storyteller in the traditional sense. Iokanaan, in the vein of Hayden White and Michel de Certeau, is a storyteller who is also a *historian* and a *prophet*. Iokanaan's knowledge of the past and the future precipitate the present action of the play. It is Iokanaan's mouth that Salome wants to kiss, for it is through his mouth that she seeks guidance about how to act in the future (because, presumably, of his knowledge of the past, as Iokanaan's knowledge of the past is more-or-less all that she hears before she seeks his advice): "Speak again, Iokanaan. Thy voice is music to mine ear...Speak again! Speak again, Iokanaan, and tell me what I must do."[34]

Iokanaan crafts his historical and teleological narratives, respectively, in mostly two rhetorical ways: (1) he asks questions and (2) he speaks in imperatives. Iokanaan's questions, for the most part, create his historical narratives. It is through his questions that the audience learns of Herodias' promiscuous past:

> Where is she who saw the images of men painted on the wall, even the images of the Chaldaeans painted with colours, and gave herself up to the lust of her eyes, and sent ambassadors into the land of Chaldaea?...Where is she who gave herself unto the Captains of Assyria, who have baldricks on their loins, and crown of many colours on their heads? Where is she who

hath given herself to the young men of the Egyptians, who are clothed in fine linen and hyacinth, whose shields are of gold, whose helmets are of silver, whose bodies are mighty?[35]

The curious thing about the fact that, via Iokanaan, history (i.e., the past) is told in the form of questions, especially in questions about location, is that what has transpired cannot be pinned down with the certainty of the corresponding grammar; however, but despite his prophetic power, what Iokanaan commands Salome to do (through imperatives) both now and in the future has more-or-less the opposite effect on Salome. The force of Iokanaan's desired future action causes Salome to want exactly what Iokanaan finds so undesirable: "Back, daughter of Sodom! Touch me not."[36]

In short, the storyteller—Iokanaan—cannot control how the narratives he casts will be used. And this is Wilde's point. Iokanaan, in order to be an effective storyteller, must remove his own desires about what he wants from his audience. The question mark, not exactly grammatically but metaphorically, shows Iokanaan's uncertainty of how to incorporate history so that it does not repeat again. In effect, Iokanaan indirectly makes history repeat itself (as stated above Iokanaan's pronouncements have an effect that is opposite to what Iokanaan desires), and the second time around is more sinister than the first: the erotic desires of Herodias become the deviant, perverse, and morbid desires of Salome. Iokanaan dies because he inserts his own desires into his desired narrative of the future (something questionable anyway for a prophet who seems to have some knowledge of the future but cannot see how his own actions affect that future). Iokanaan uses historical narratives to teach indirectly his own morality. Wilde chooses this story, in a sense, because the moral-historical narrative told by Iokanaan (however, natural it is to cast history as such, via White) reeks of a *passive* didacticism. Wilde's own detached storytelling or translation of this historical/biblical story is meant to contrast Iokanaan's didacticism in favor of a type of *active* didacticism much more like Brecht's that forces the audience, through alienation and detachment from desire and emotion, to learn, on their own, how to act in the future.

Salome in performance

Although I focus here on one production that was not explicitly billed as a Brechtian production of the play, in general, in terms of the history of the performance of the play (and the opera), the more recent the production, the more overtly Brechtian the performances were (though none were advertised as Brechtian productions of *Salome*).[37]

It would be hard to think of any other word to describe the production history of Oscar Wilde's *Salome* than opulent. The work has been famously adapted as an opera and a ballet, and Peter Brook's production of Strauss's opera, with Dalí-designed sets and a dress made out of thousands of peacock feathers, is simply the most extreme example of the design excess that has been brought to both the play and its adaptations. Such opulence, which has at times reached decadent levels in the minds of some critics, has long been associated with Wilde. Consequently, some have thought of Wilde as an apolitical playwright. However, several recent productions have rejected opulence and explored the social politics implicit in the play. In Estelle Parson's *Salome: The Reading*, this trend towards anti-opulent and political production develops into a feminist critique and an exploration of the theatre's potential to subvert received hierarchies.

Salome: The Reading is a collaboration of historic significance, pairing director Estelle Parson, famed for her multiethnic and multilingual productions, with Yukio Tsuji, who for twenty years has been the house composer at the edgy "international" La MaMa Experimental Theatre Club. From the moment I first saw the stage at the Ethel Barrymore Theatre in New York City, I knew this would be a radical departure from past productions. The set was rather bare; clusters of black music stands and wood and metal folding chairs sat close to the audience, stageleft and stageright. In the center of the stage, a slightly raised "T" platform formed the throne room for Herod. Another square platform, downstage and raised only one step from the ground just like Herod's throne room, suggested Iokanaan's cistern. Yukio Tsuji performed with all of his instruments stageleft in full view of the audience. Equally noticeable was the absence of the stairway where, at the end of the play, Herod stops mid-ascension and pronounces the death sentence for "that woman!"

The actors emerged scripts in hand. This was not necessarily surprising, given that the production was billed as a "Reading." However, this was not a strict reading. Or rather, the production played with the conventions of the reading to produce both critical detachment and empathy in the audience. The actors often sat scripts in hand or stood before the music stands. At other times, however, they were mobile and sometimes delivered lines off-book. Frequently the actors delivered their lines to the audiences in the manner of a reading, other times the actors created intimate moments between characters. The Dance of the Seven Veils, as performed by Marisa Tomei, was profoundly theatrical and arresting. She instantly switched from a reader into character, performed a frenzied, erotic dance—ripping off her top off at the end of the dance and leaving herself exposed—and than just as quickly returned to her role as reader. With the simple gesture of picking the script back up, Tomei broke the emotional spell, foregrounding actor over character.

In that one dance, Tomei dramatized the dialectical relation between actor and character, allowing the audience to see how the actor's personal agenda and politics emerge in the creation of her art. Moments before the dance, with her script in hand, Tomei foregrounded her own status as an actor distinct from the character she presented. This bifurcation was strategically subverted during the emotional dance, as when Salome made eye contact with Herod, and then reestablished, as when the actress suddenly, very glaringly condemned the audience—the voyeurs—with a conscious stare. In the process, the audience was allowed to see multiple characters—Wilde's Salome, Parson's Salome, Tomei's Salome, the historical Salome, and Marisa Tomei—all conflated into one body. The fluid boundaries between actor and character in this production allowed for a social commentary on the objectified woman and the power and powerlessness that voyeurism bestows on her. After that decisive glance, Wilde's *Salome* was changed forever.

In Parson's production, it became easy to see how Wilde presented his characters as actors in their own right, potential beasts of hierarchical sabotage and indeterminacy. Like Patrick Dupond's Salome in his ballet, who "was not a boy or a girl but in between,"[38] Tomei, Al Pacino, and the rest of the talented cast were not actors or characters but "in between." The audience experienced a metaphoric puppet show, with the stage and all of its devices, and many of its intentions, becoming transparent, like the strings in Kohl's assertion that the characters are "puppet-like." This Brechtian turn in Wilde's *Salome* is extremely significant. Estelle Parson's suggestive reading of *Salome* turns the usually eerie, fable-like, opulent, full-blown production into a subtly subversive and intentionally detached reading. To my knowledge, there has been no real discussion that ever really brought Brecht and Wilde under the same lens. Hopefully this latest productions will help make it possible to bring two major writers into a previously hardly imagined dialogue, possibly eroding the strict division between the apolitical and the opulence of Wilde's theatre and the political anti-decadence of Brecht's theatre.

Wilde: the translator

Salome is a historically relative modern history play in the vein of Brecht as can be attested to by its production history. However, its fairy tale–like quality, its sense of happening in a far-off, distant time and place, also suggests much more about Wilde's imagination of what biblical Judea was like—and more about what his own society was like—than about biblical Judea itself. *Salome*, then, is a Symbolist portrait of biblical Judea through the eyes of a nineteenth-century Irishman, who made his home primarily in London, writing the play (while living at the time in Paris) in French.

Ian Andrew MacDonald investigates the influence that French biblical translations had on Wilde's word choices in *Salome* and how, through Wilde's imperfect but acceptable control of the French language, Wilde uses the French language to create moments in the text that are essentially untranslatable and are not found in the English version of the play. MacDonald notes, possibly due to Wilde's seeming predilection for writing in French like one would speak and for his smaller French vocabulary and inability to use complex syntax, that Wilde uses phrases such as "enfin" ("after all") sixteen times and "On dirait" ("one would say") fourteen times. MacDonald suggests that this repetition in the French text is "the primary reason why the English text has its unique style that is so different from the style of his comedies of manners written in English," featuring "linguistic repetitiveness and simplicity that is hypnotic and musical in a way that Wilde's prose in the comedies is not."[39] Furthermore, while much of the style of Salome in English sounds like the King James Bible and Peter Cogin suggests that Wilde referred to a 1667 French version of the bible, MacDonald argues that Wilde most likely looked to other French translations of the bible, as well.[40] Noting some peculiarities in the French text, MacDonald zeros in on Wilde's use of *tu* and *vous*, the singular and plural "you": while Wilde's French text reads like modern, standard French, Wilde's translation into English—using "thou," "thee," and "thy"—"call[s] to mind Middle English and the King James Version of the Bible."[41] MacDonald concludes: "Wilde shows that he viewed translation as an opportunity to make editorial changes normally beyond the purview of literary translators, shifting the tone of his English *Salome* into a far more archaic style."[42] MacDonald explains why Wilde may have shifted tones: "The Salome myth was a commonly used motif in late nineteenth-century French artistic ad literary culture, whereas it was more alien and foreign to an English audience."[43] In other words, the portrayal of biblical Judeans speaking King James biblical English (or Middle English) says a lot about Wilde's late-nineteenth-century English audience and Wilde's own perception of his English audience.

Before Wilde was a successful writer, however, Wilde was, first, a successful classicist. While at Trinity College, Dublin, Wilde won the Berkeley Gold Medal for Greek and worked with his mentor J. P. Mahaffy on Mahaffy's *Social Life in Greece*. Wilde, then, received a B.A. in Classical Moderations and Literae Humaniores (Greats) at Oxford University, studying the Latin and Greek language, and Roman and Greek history and philosophy, respectively. Wilde, as is well-known, was greatly influenced by his mentor at Oxford, Walter Pater. About Pater's *Studies in the History of the Renaissance*, Wilde used to call it "my golden book,"[44] and he loved Pater's first book, *Marius the Epicurean*, about a young Roman.

Though Wilde was extremely familiar with the bible himself and would have almost-certainly known the two versions of the beheading of St. John the Baptist in the bible (Matt. 14:3–12[45] and Mark 6:17–29[46]), it is very likely that it was Pater who indirectly planted the seeds for *Salome* in Wilde's head. According to Richard Ellmmann:

> Pater lent Wilde a copy of *Trois Contes*, just published in Paris. In this work of "the sinless master whom mortals call Flaubert," as Wilde described him in a letter, were the stories of St Julien, Herodias, and St John. These particularly impressed Wilde, who thereafter began to compose his skeptical revisions of Biblical narratives. He borrowed from Flaubert also the Greek form of John's name (Iokanaan).[47]

Christopher S. Nassaar also, in his article "Pater in Wilde's *The Happy Prince and Other Tales* and *A House of Pomegranates*," discusses Pater's influence on Wilde's literary career:

> Oscar Wilde's mature literary career began in 1886, when he wrote "Lord Arthur Savile's Crime" then followed it up with "The Canterville Ghost" and the fairy tales of *The Happy Prince and Other Tales* and *A House of Pomegranates*. These tales reveal many influences—Hans Christian Andersen, Blake, Carlyle—but Pater is a chief influence on many of them. In *De Profundis*, Wilde wrote of *Marius The Epicurean* that in it "Pater seeks to reconcile the artistic life with the life of religion in the deep, sweet and austere sense of the word. But Marius is little more than a spectator: an ideal spectator indeed,... yet a spectator merely, and perhaps a little too much occupied with the comeliness of the vessels of the Sanctuary to notice

that it is the Sanctuary of Sorrow that he is gazing at" (Letters 476). In many of the fairy tales, Wilde's concern is exactly that of Pater's in Marius—to blend Christianity and the artistic life or aestheticism—with the difference that the emotional content is higher and impresses us more strongly that we are in "the Sanctuary of Sorrow." In others, he is more concerned with the Conclusion to *The Renaissance*, with its insistent advice that we should devote our lives to the private enjoyment of the best objects of art—advice which he strongly rejects.[48]

Alex Murray also writes about the complex relationship and extent of Pater's influence on Wilde. Murray argues:

> This movement towards an ontological aesthetic is responsible for taking the logic of Paterian aesthetics to their inevitable conclusion, one which Wilde saw as the most effect challenge to the hegemonic Victorian culture. It also marks the point at which art, in its challenge to the social mores, denied any obligation to challenge models of social organisation, rejecting the earlier Utopian art of Romanticism. In this self-conscious rejection of the social, we see the beginnings of a cultural politics in which a schism between the realm of the aesthetic and the life-world develop; in which art's engagement with the social and political is one of rejection, not of engagement.[49]

Though set in 161–177 A.C.E., over 100 years after the events surrounding St. John the Baptist, and in Rome, not in Judea, Pater's *Marius The Epicurean* displays some interesting links to Wilde's *Salome*. Pater's use of classical and historical texts, which display an *intertextuality* (something that Kees de Vries suggests Wilde displays in *Salome*[50]), and Pater's suggestion that Marius' time of change and uncertainty was similar to Pater's own era, can be found, both directly and indirectly, in Wilde's *Salome*.

Transporting his audience to a far-away place, biblical Judea, Wilde is able to have his audience "live through" a despotic society. Unlike Marius, who Nassaar argues is the "ideal spectator" of a time of change, Salome is an *active participant*, however unlikely her ability to affect change may be. In Salome's clearly hyper-classed society, Salome moves in-between different worlds and spheres. This in-between character that Wilde creates in Salome, especially when juxtaposed with *The Importance of Being Earnest*, displays (to disagree with Murray) Wilde's *engagement* with his own society. But just as importantly, Wilde's *Salome* forces the audience to engage with their own society in shaping a future. While it is Salome who is the active participant, it is the audience who is the active spectator, trying to reconceptualize a world where Salomé's "Sanctuary of Sorrow"—the sorrow of *being* and *not being* Salomé—comes into contact with Wilde's own world (especially if Salomé is conceived as a bunburyist like Algernon and Jack in *The Importance of Being Earnest*).

Conclusion: *always* Salomé

Why did Oscar Wilde specifically choose the Salomé story? I think the clue can be found in Salomé's *presence* in the bible. As mentioned earlier, while there is a historical record of Salomé in Josephus' *Antiquities of the Jews*, Salomé both exists and does not exist in the bible. Because Salomé is unnamed in the bible, she is indefinite and amorphous. However, given the Zen Buddhist idea that once you name something you kill it, Salomé is also full of possibilities since she is unnamed. Therefore, when Herod proclaims, "Kill that woman!" Herod may have killed the woman, but he did not kill the idea. In *Salomé*, the pronouncement of "Kill that woman!" suggests that by the end of the play who Salomé is still does not match how she is perceived. And, in this way, *Salomé* is a tragedy. However, by the grace of the playwright's pen in the final stage directions—"*Salomé, daughter of Herodias, Princess of Judea*"—Wilde shows that he both *perceives* and *knows* Salomé as one and the same person (and, thus, the audience does, as well). In this sense, Salomé, her story, and her paradox (the same paradoxes shared by the masses in Wilde's society) live on and will be explored forever, bringing the historical and biblical *Salomé* eternally from Wilde's present into both his and our future.

Notes

1   Kohl, *Oscar Wilde*, 193.
2   Ibid.
3   Tillis, "The Actor Occluded," 109.
4   Quigley, "Realism and Symbolism in Oscar Wilde's Salomé," 108.
5   Donohue, "*Salome* and the Wildean Art of Symbolist Theatre," 86.
6   Wilde, "Salomé," *Oscar Wilde*, 66.
7   Ibid. 75.
8   Ibid. 70.
9   "Penumbra," *The Oxford English Dictionary*, 2nd ed., 1989.
10 Wilde, "Salomé," 77.

11 This information is from Joseph Donohue's personal notes on the Rosenbach *Salome*, 1.2v.
12 Wilde, "Salome," 91.
13 Ibid.
14 McAuley, *Space in Performance*, 98.
15 Ibid. 68.
16 "Stay," *Oxford English Dictionary*, 2nd ed. 1989.
17 Wilde, "Salome," 72.
18 Ibid. 85.
19 Ibid. 91.
20 Ibid.
21 Kohl, *Oscar Wilde*, 186.
22 Donohue, "*Salome* and the Wildean Art of Symbolist Theatre," 84.
23 Brecht, *Brecht on Theatre*, , 190.
24 Wilde, *Complete Letters*, 197.
25 Ibid. 199.
26 Brecht, *Brecht on Theatre*, 192.
27 I found Steven Swann Jones' introduction in his book, *The Fairy Tale: The Magic Mirror of Imagination*, particularly helpful in categorizing the genres within folk narratives.
28 Kohl, *Oscar Wilde*, 52.
29 Zipes, *Fairy Tale as Myth*, 4.
30 Ibid. 6.
31 Ibid. 9.
32 Ibid. 10.
33 Ibid. 9.
34 Wilde, "Salome," 72.
35 Ibid. 71.
36 Ibid. 73.
37 I. *King's Hall, 1906* Although the King's Hall production of *Salome* in Covent Garden, London in 1906 could not, of course, have predicted Brecht's aesthetic manifestos for the theatre, the review by Max Meyerfield reads as though this was a self-declared Brechtian production of *Salome*: "The stage was left ridiculously bare, and never for a moment produced the illusion of the terrace outside of Herod's banqueting hall...the Dance of the Seven Veils was executed with all of the propriety of a British governess" (Tanitch, *Oscar Wilde on Stage and Screen*, 144). Why had the director, C. S. Ricketts, opted for a stage like this? Richard Allen Cave's comments about this performance are insightful: "[Rickett's] objective seems always to bring an audience into an enhanced awareness of the inner dynamics of the action which constitute the subject...subtle use of design to shape an audience's sensitivity of response" ("Wilde Designs," 179). Cave goes on to explain that Brecht was exploring similar territory to that of Ricketts (181).

II. *Royal Opera House, 1949* Although this was not the first production of Richard Strauss's *Salome*—which premiered in Dresden in 1905— this production in London may have been one of the more alienating performances, given the designer: Salvador Dali. "Salvador Dali provided a background of gigantic peacock feathers, yards and yards of scarlet nylon net, huge spiked shields. Herodias could barely move inside her head-dress and collar. The designs caused an uproar" (Tanitch, *Oscar Wilde on Stage and Screen*, 165). Certainly, these designs ensured that this production could not be a "slice of life." Instead the imaginary world created a Brechtian dream: "The one important point for the spectators in these houses is that they should be able to swap a contradictory world for a consistent one, one that they scarcely know for one of which they can dream" (Brecht, *Brecht on Theatre*, 188). Furthermore, as the director, Peter Brook, noted: "The aim is a musical one. This *Salome* is designed much more for singers" (Tanitch, *Oscar Wilde on Stage and Screen*, 174). For Brecht, "... music can make its point in a number of ways and with full independence, and can react in its own manner to the subjects dealt with; at the same time it can also quite simply help to lend variety to the entertainment" (Brecht, *Brecht on Theatre*, 203). Oscar Wilde's play lent itself beautifully to an adaptation for opera.

III. *Paris, 1973* In his "A Short Organum for the Theatre," Brecht discusses another acting method (previously unmentioned in this article) for alienating the audience: "If the part is played by somebody of the opposite sex the sex of the character will be more clearly brought out; if it is played by a comedian, whether comically or tragically, it will gain fresh aspects" (Brecht, *Brecht on Theatre*, 197). This all-male production in 1973 in Paris accomplished this very feat.

IV. *City Centre Theatre, 1985* Presented by the Ballet of the 20th Century, this adaptation into ballet of *Salome* in New York was best described by Patrick Dupond (who played Salome) in an interview: "Seduction is pushed until destruction. It is inspired by Kabuki and Oscar Wilde. I have to act as much as I dance. *I'm not a boy or a girl but in between*. It's very strange and very tricky" (Tanitch, *Oscar Wilde on Stage and Screen*, 180, my emphasis). Here we revisit the idea of liminality. This portrayal of Salome makes the character indefinite and highlights the same impossibility of acting that puppetry demonstrates. In addition, the Asiatic quality of the performance (its Kabuki inspiration) fits well with Brechtian theatre.

V. *The Gate Theatre, 1988* Richard Alan Cave wrote with great insight about Steven Berkhoff's *Salome*, which first premiered at The Gate Theatre in Dublin in 1988, was transferred to the Royal National Theatre in London (1989), then played at the Edinburgh Festival (1989) and subsequently at the Spoleto Festival in Charleston, South Carolina (1990). In the 1989 production at the Royal National Theatre in London, Steven Berkhoff played Herod. Cave writes this about Berkhoff's production:

> This was not costume drama or biblical spectacle, nor was it a sensational indulgence in kinky sexuality (there was no sensationalism of any kind: even Salome's dance was a *mimed* striptease in which no clothes were actually removed). Berkhoff showed *Salome* to be a political play with a rigorous metaphysical edge to its satirical intent. To do this, he relentlessly subverted all possible expectations an audience might bring to the performance, established through revivals over the last two decades... and a consequence of this was that Berkhoff restored to the play its considerable subversive potential. (Cave, "Wilde Designs," 182–183)

With Berkhoff's production, *Salome* has become a play that does not follow Wilde's dictum of "art for art's sake," but instead can be read as a subversively political play. Furthermore, the act of miming the removal of Salome's clothes constitutes a Brechtian showing: there is an obvious transparency in this production between acting and action.

38 Tanitch, *Oscar Wilde on Stage and Screen*, 180.
39 Ian Andrew MacDonald, "Oscar Wilde as a French Writer, 4.
40 Ibid.
41 Ibid. 6.
42 Ibid. 17.
43 Ibid.
44 Ellmann, *Oscar Wilde at Oxford*, 12.
45 Matt. 14:3 For Herod had seized John and bound him and put him in prison, for the sake of Hero'di-as, his brother Philip's wife; 14:4 because John said to him, "It is not lawful for you to have her." 14:5 And though he wanted to put him to death, he feared the people, because they held him to be a prophet. 14:6 But when Herod's birthday came, the daughter of Hero'di-as danced before the company, and pleased Herod, 14:7 so that he promised with an oath to give her whatever she might ask. 14:8 Prompted by her mother, she said, "Give me the head of John the Baptist here on a platter." 14:9 And the king was sorry; but because of his oaths and his guests he commanded it to be given; 14:10 he sent and had John beheaded in the prison, 14:11 and his head was brought on a platter and given to the girl, and she brought it to her mother. 14:12 And his disciples came and took the body and buried it; and they went and told Jesus.
46 Mark 6:17 For Herod had sent and seized John, and bound him in prison for the sake of Hero'di-as, his brother Philip's wife; because he had married her. 6:18 For John said to Herod, "It is not lawful for you to have your brother's wife." 6:19 And Hero'di-as had a grudge against him, and wanted to kill

him. But she could not, 6:20 For Herod feared John, knowing that he was a righteous and holy man, and kept him safe. When he heard him, he was much perplexed; and yet he heard him gladly. 6:21 But an opportunity came when Herod on his birthday gave a banquet for his courtiers and officers and the leading men of Galilee. 6:22 For when Hero'di-as' daughter came in and danced, she pleased Herod and his guests; and the king said to the girl, "Ask me for whatever you wish, and I will grant it." 6:23 And he vowed to her, "Whatever you ask me, I will give you, even half of my kingdom." 6:24 And she went out, and said to her mother, "What shall I ask?" And she said, "The head of John the baptizer." 6:25 And she came in immediately with haste to the king, and asked, saying, "I want you to give me at once the head of John the Baptist on a platter." 6:26 And the king was exceedingly sorry; but because of his oaths and his guests he did not want to break his word to her. 6:27 And immediately the king sent a soldier of the guard and gave orders to bring his head. He went and beheaded him in the prison, 6:28 And brought his head on a platter, and gave it to the girl; and the girl gave it to her mother. 6:29 When his disciples heard of it, they came and took his body, and laid it in a tomb.

47 Ellmann, *Oscar Wilde*, 84.
48 Nassaar, "Pater in Wilde's *The Happy Prince and Other Tales* and *A House of Pomegranates*," 142.
49 A. Murray, "Acquiescing into a Facile Orthodoxy? 326.
50 See de Vries, "Intertextuality and Intermediality," 235–255.

3
Galileo's Narrative: Translating History's "Conditions" in Brecht's *Life of Galileo*

Abstract: *Chapter 3 examines Brecht's understanding of the need to convey "conditions" from one time to another, from one culture to another. Focusing on the telescope as the central metaphor and agent of change in the play, I argue that Brecht models the structure of the play after it: creating a telos-shaped arc that forces the audience to consider their future actions. Thought about in this way, and juxtaposing it with notions of history, I argue that Brecht forces his audience to suffer what Alasdair MacIntyre calls an "epistemological crisis," by pitting historical narratives against one another. The resolution of this created epistemological crisis gets to the very heart of Brecht's notion of what epic theatre attempts to do.*

Bennett, Y. Michael. *Narrating the Past through Theatre: Four Crucial Texts.* New York: Palgrave Macmillan, 2013. DOI: 10.1057/9781137275424.

> Walls and spheres and immobility! For two thousand years people have believed that the sun and all the stars of heaven rotate around mankind. Pope, cardinals, princes, professors, captains, merchants, fishwives and school kids thought they were sitting motionless inside this crystal sphere. But now we are breaking out of it, Andrea, at full speed. Because the old days are over and this is a new time.
>
> —Galileo, *Life of Galileo*[1]
>
> The universe has lost its centre overnight, and woken up to find it has countless centres. So that each one can now be seen as the centre, or none at all. Suddenly there is a lot of room.
>
> —Galileo, *Life of Galileo*[2]
>
> In order to unearth society's laws of motion this method treats social situations as processes, and traces out all their inconsistencies. It regards nothing as existing in so far as it changes, in other words is in disharmony with itself.
>
> —Bertolt Brecht, *A Short Organum for the Theatre*[3]
>
> The laws of motion of a society are not to be demonstrated by "perfect examples," for "imperfection" (inconsistency) is an initial part of motion and the thing moved.
>
> —Bertolt Brecht, *A Short Organum for the Theatre*[4]

It is well-known among Bertolt Brecht scholars that the original title of Brecht's *Life of Galileo* was *The Earth Moves*. The above epigraphs attest to Brecht's fascination with *movement* and *motion*, not just in *Galileo* but in Brecht's most well-known theoretical piece of writing, *A Short Organum for the Theatre*. (Given that Brecht discusses Galileo/*Galileo* in seven of his numbered sections in *A Short Organum*, it is not so far-fetched to juxtapose these two texts by Brecht.) But putting these passages into a working dialog exposes something curious: while Galileo destroys one consistent, "perfect" system (the Ptolemaic universe), he creates (or explains) another consistent, "perfect" system (the Copernican universe, with a system of *now-understood-to-be-basically* predictable, consistent orbits). There are, then, just two differences between the systems: (1) the Copernican system incorporates movement (unlike the system of "immobility" found in the Ptolemaic system), and (2) there is no inherent "centre" to the Copernican system (versus a very clear center in the Ptolemaic system, earth). Do these two differences in the Copernican system address the "inconsistencies" that Brecht wants to expose? In general, no.

Of course, it is also well-known among (not just Brecht, but) modern drama scholars that Brecht was preoccupied with history. Brecht's concern was in portraying the historically relative:

> We must drop our habit of taking the different social structures of past periods, stripping them of everything that makes them different; so that they all look more or less like our own, which then acquires from this process a certain air of having been there all along, in other words of permanence pure and simple. Instead we must leave them their distinguishing marks and keep their impermanence always before our eyes, so that our own period can be seen to be impermanent too...If we ensure that our characters on the stage are moved by social impulses and that these differ according to the period, then we make it harder for our spectator to identify himself with them. He cannot simply feel: that's how I would act, but at most can say: if I had lived under those circumstances.

It is in thinking about Brecht's presentation of history and portraying the historically relative and his fascination concerning movement that maybe we can understand what Brecht was doing in *Galileo* and why proving the Copernican universe was consistent with Brecht's *modus operandi*.

Movement and history, on the surface, appear to be at odds. History is generally relegated to an objective past that seems immobile, immutable, complete, and dead. But as I discussed Michel de Certeau's assertions about history in the Introduction, history (or at least in the *telling* of history, the narrative form of history that Hayden White observes, which is the only way we *know* history) is, however, quite alive and in constant motion. If Certeau's and White's observations about history and its production are taken together, then history is mutable, not for the present—for our socially determined narratives and sense of our current time are somewhat set—but for the unpredictable future, where its sense of ruptures, beginnings, and ends will be determined by the future's current situation and sense of narrative form.

It is in this manner that Brecht is able to reconcile the above epigraphs. Brechtian acting technique, where the actor comments on his or her character, makes the historically relative always *adaptable* to the future (and the future's unpredictable social arrangements). Thus, different social conditions are understood by different narratives. And it is—actually, rather—the juxtaposition of two narratives (from two different historical conditions) and how these two narratives expose the imprecision and inconsistency of both narratives that produces the alienation effect (A-effect) for the audience.[5] The audience exposed to the alienation effect experiences, what Alasdair MacIntyre has called, an "epistemological crisis." MacIntyre suggests that one experiences an epistemological crisis when one encounters the relationship of *seems* to *is*.[6] When a person's culturally determined schemata, or worldview, is thrown into question by unveiling or discovering new information that contradicts this person's schemata, throwing this person into an epistemological crisis, this person, in order to resolve the epistemological crisis, must create a new narrative.[7] And this—the forced creation by the audience of new narratives based upon presenting a contradictory world of *seems* to *is*—is Brecht's entire point of epic theatre. Thus, *Galileo* examines the point in human history where narrative and the idea of motion intersect: forcing the audience to be aware of conflicting narratives; forcing the audience to realize that their own narratives about the world are just socially and culturally constructed (i.e., artificial, in the broad sense, and human-made, in the more general sense); and forcing the audience to accept that both narratives and society is not a given and is not unchangeable.

Richard J. Beckley sees history playing a key role in understanding Bertolt Brecht's *Life of Galileo*. Using techniques of epic theatre in *Galileo*, Brecht, according to Beckley, breaks down the Aristotelian feeling of tragic inevitability by attacking the impression of strict causality and the links between the incidents in the play.[8] In showing each stage of the action, Brecht suggests that there are various possibilities for development and reasons for a chain of events, not just an inevitable, causal one that necessarily leads to a tragic conclusion.[9] Addressing the Aristotelian tragic hero, Beckley argues that Brecht supplants "the tragic view of man as a helpless pawn in the hands of fate, for a view of man socially conditioned in his actions, forced into a tragic situation by social conditions."[10] Beckley suggests that the audience experiences a tragic outcome for one individual caused by the malfunctioning of society, but the audience is also shown that society does not have to operate in this unsatisfactory way.[11]

Joseph Dial continues this line of thinking and argues that in *Galileo*, Brecht juxtaposes two Galileos. Brecht uses elements of Aristotelian drama to dramatize the Galileo portrayed by history books, where middle-class historians attempted to make Galileo's actions understandable, showing that he was a hero in the story of human progress.[12] But Brecht, as Dial asserts, also uses non-Aristotelian forms of representation from epic theatre: for example, the ballad singer ties Galileo's teachings with social revolution (in the 1938 version).[13] Dial suggests that the effect of this juxtaposition is that the "concept of continuous motivation wherein each action is explainable in terms of what went before, as itself transitory, historical, and limited," found in an Aristotelian representation of Galileo's life was a middle-class way to observe history, unable to reproduce the contradictions in life (unlike Brecht's own "non-Aristotelian 'distortion'").[14]

Dial reads *Galileo*'s dramatization through the tension in history between objective history, what happened, and transmitted history, the description of what happened. Brecht takes the Galileo of history books (transmitted history) and turns it into objective history to demonstrate an episode in Galileo's life; thus, *Galileo* shows how constructing Galileo in an Aristotelian manner is a product of a particular way of viewing history (which is limited by the historical circumstances).[15] On the other hand, for Brecht, "Galileo's recanting had to be accepted as fact, but also a decision, under different circumstances, could have been different... Had Galileo considered his own actions from the dialectical viewpoint, and seen the elements of class struggle in the Inquisition, he could have chosen a different course and alleviated some of the problems that now plague the twentieth century."[16] Dial is able to conclude from this argument that Brecht perceived recognizing history as a middle-class struggle to be the first progressive step after Fascism; thus, it was necessary to reread history books in order to see their middle-class perception of history, juxtaposing this perception against the proletariat, dialectical perspective of revolutionary discontinuity (the only perspective that Brecht thought could defeat Fascism).[17]

Scholarship surrounding Bertolt Brecht's *Life of Galileo* has centered around three main strands: (1) historicity and authenticity of the plot,[18] (2) the Aristotelian structure of the plot,[19] and (3) Brecht's three versions of the play.[20] This chapter aims at bringing these three scholarly dialogs into conversation (especially the first two), extending the arguments started by Beckley and Dial, by examining the structure of the play in relation to the historical arc of the *telos*. If we think about Brecht employing a historical *telos*, instead of thinking that Brecht fell back into Aristotelian drama (and, thus, weakening the message of the play, since an Aristotelian structure contrasts with Brecht's theories of the theatre that are clearly demonstrated in the "Brechtian" structure of epic theater), we are able to see how Brecht was able to create a modern history play and strengthen his call to *action* by incorporating the future into the past and present.

But it is the subject matter itself in this play that gives the history, in a sense, its shape and power. Galileo proves Copernican cosmology, overturning the Ptolemaic system, with a telescope. Telescope comes from "telos" and "scopeo,"[21] with *telos* being the "end, purpose, ultimate object or aim."[22] The telescope, then, becomes both the agent of change and the metaphor of the play. The Ptolemaic system cast the earth in the center of eight rings, or crystal spheres. The telescope, in the hands of Galileo, allowed mankind to "[break] out of it."[23] It was by looking telescopically that Galileo could project the future movements of the earth and planets. Our (the earth's) past movements and present position in the universe, then, determine our future course. For Brecht, exposing our past movements (our history and past historical condition) to our present (present condition), allows humans "the courage to…soar through space without support," soaring without support in a manner not simply charted out by a set of stellar coordinates.[24] Maybe this is why Brecht originally named the play, *The Earth Moves*. The shape of the play, its Aristotelian arc, does not lessen Brecht's message or suggest that this play called into question Brecht's notions of epic theatre and theories about the stage. Instead, the play mirrors the central image of the play, the telescope, and takes the audience on a *telos*-shaped arc where the audience must measure both the distance between their past and present condition and the movement of bodies within each historical condition to determine their *own* future course of *action*. While *Life of Galileo* might be Brecht's most classically structured play on the surface, if Brecht wants his audience to spring into action, *Life of Galileo* is certainly structured, more so than any other of his plays, to accomplish just that.

Brecht's epistemological crises

The three versions of *Galileo*

An observation by Betty Nance Weber that Brecht displayed a "systematic, rational pattern of relating history in reverse, i.e. from 1938 backward,"[25] is important to the fact that *Galileo* was written three times. Weber notes that Brecht explores the past, progressing from history in *Galileo*, to the picaresque in *Mother Courage and her Children*, to the fairy tale in *The Good Person of Szechwan*, and finally to legend in *The Caucasian*

Chalk Circle.²⁶ It is interesting to note, however, his society's situation when Brecht finished each play. He finished (the first version of) *Galileo* in 1938 when living in Denmark before there were signs of it being invaded. He finished *Mother Courage* after Germany invaded Poland in 1939. He finished *Szechwan* in the United States, near the beginning of their involvement in WWII. And he finished *Chalk Circle* in 1944 in the United States at a time when the tides of WWII had begun to turn (for the Allies and against the Axis). In some sense, to Brecht, the world must have seemed to progressively lose sight of history (and the lessons garnered from it) and any objectivity that history offered. Posts-WWII, Brecht was able to return to history (rewriting the "American" version of *Galileo*), maybe hoping that this time the world could learn from the disasters of fascism: that fascism was human-made by society, and that a new world order that emerged near the end and after WWII (in part) was what drove fascism from Europe.

More specifically with *Galileo*, it is very significant that Brecht rewrote Galileo three times, during crucial years in history, as John Willett and Ralph Manheim point out: "Hitler's triumphs in 1938, the dropping of the first nuclear bomb in 1945, the death of Stalin in 1953."²⁷ Willett and Manheim also note how the conditions of work were different each time, each version having its own style: the first version in a measure stylish but down-to-earth German; the second rewritten for an Anglo-English audience; and the third, put back into German to combine the best of both of the first two texts.²⁸ Besides Brecht's continued concerns with world politics, during the writing of the first version, he lived in Denmark (a generally neutral country); during the writing of the second version, he lived in the United States (who many thought saved the world from fascism); and during the writing of the third version, he lived in Germany (specifically communist East Berlin, where the death of Stalin would be notable). Thus, I argue, that his style was a reflection of each of these society's sense of world and historical narratives (and how each country fit into these narratives). In a sense, Brecht had to rewrite *Galileo*, as each historical condition (1938 Denmark, 1945 United States, and 1953 East Berlin) suggested to Brecht that a new narrative was needed. Brecht, himself, (most likely subconsciously) underwent his own epistemological crises during these drastically different historical conditions, and each version of *Galileo* was the manifestation of Brecht's newly constructed narrative.

Brecht's *Life of Galileo*

Galileo's narrative

The play begins in Galileo's *"rather wretched study,"* where geometry is used to describe Galileo's "wretched" financial situation: the milkman will "circle" the house and the bailiff will choose the "shortest" "distance between two points."[29] However, this—in the mode of the Brechtian contradiction—alerts the audience immediately to what becomes one of the central rhetorical metaphors of the play. Brecht juxtaposes the perfectness of the circle and the pure logic of choosing the shortest distance between two points with the wretchedness of conditions, both Galileo's and his society's. In a sense, Brecht wants the audience to remember that such perfect systems, such as geometry, do exist even in a larger imperfect system (i.e., Galileo's society).

Brecht immediately complicates the notion, however, when Galileo shows Andrea the wooden model of the Ptolemaic universe. The Ptolemaic model shows precision and logic (with its ever-larger concentric rings), and while it is not actually true, it is logical to the humans in Galileo's society. Galileo's subsequent wax poetic on the earth "rolling cheerfully around the sun" and how the "universe has lost its centre overnight," again, while true, frankly makes Galileo sound like a manic, mad scientist, not the "teacher of mathematics at Padua" who apparently teaches Andrea the foundations of geometric logic.[30] And, thus, right away we uncover Galileo's miscalculation that leads to his downfall: much like Danton in chapter 1, who could not craft a more favorable translation of history than Robespierre, Galileo does not know how to craft a narrative appropriate for his contemporary society, or in other words, he cannot adequately translate an appropriate scientific narrative to his audience (whom he clearly does not understand). Galileo's failure, then, is not realizing that one narrative, one translation, of truth does not necessarily translate well to all audiences: *a translator translates a narrative for a specific audience.*

Wolfgang Sohlich discusses Galileo's use of the telescope through the dialectic of distance and proximity: by Galileo pointing the telescope toward the stars, and looking at his own world from the distance of planetary constellations, Brecht explores the possibility of a qualitative transformation of human life that can be lived fully in the present, intimate with the object world.[31] While I do believe what Sohlich says, the problem that Sohlich does not address is that while

DOI: 10.1057/9781137275424

Galileo does look *out* to the stars and then the reverse, going from the stars *back* to the human realm, Galileo, rather, while doing the first (i.e., looking at the stars) well, cannot *effectively* communicate the latter (i.e., relating the stars back to humans so that humans can take in his teachings). Galileo, I argue, to his demise, crafts his scientific narrative like the metaphorical object of the play that is the agent of change that is the subject of scene two, the telescope. As I wrote earlier, Galileo sees the world telescopically, pointing to the *telos*. But while Galileo, a mathematics professor, can connect the dots, connecting the "distance between two points" in the "shortest" possible manner, Galileo assumes that everyone is equally equipped and in a place in life to want to connect the dots between the observer and what is telescopically observed. The *problem* with the telescope, if you will, is that it reveals to the human observer the "end" or "ultimate aim" without letting the observer see the points in-between, the steps and space needed to provide perspective.

We begin to see the narrative that Galileo creates in scene three. Speaking to Sagredo, Galileo says: "Today mankind can write in his diary: Got rid of heaven."[32] Concerning his discovery with the telescope, Galileo's narrative points not to any theories of mathematics, but to the *telos*, his "ultimate aim" of freeing the world from the "immobility" (implicitly) of religion. Galileo plays the philosopher, but he is not the most convincing one. A successful philosopher generally takes the student through a series of understandable and clear examples in order to teach his or her end goal. As discussed above, Galileo jumps more-or-less to his conclusion. Galileo should realize this as a mathematician. Mathematicians *prove* theories with equations and proofs, showing step-by-step how he or she proceeded from the problem to a solution. The solution is hard to disagree with because each step is small and based on sound mathematical logic (which is generally very hard to disagree with).

Galileo calms the storm with a practical use for the telescope when Sagredo says to the Procurator, "My dear Mr Priuli. I may not be competent to judge this instrument's value for commerce but its value for philosophy is so boundless."[33]; but as soon as the Procurator leaves, Galileo once more becomes the philosopher and theologian, jumping in one moment from stars to the absence of God:

> SAGREDO: In other words that it's just a lot of stars. Then where's God?
> GALILEO: What d'you mean?

SAGREDO: God! Where is God?
GALILEO: *angrily* Not there anyway. Any more than he'd be here on earth, suppose there were creatures out there wanting to come and look for him.
SAGREDO: So where is God?
GALILEO: I'm not a theologian. I'm a mathematician.
SAGREDO: First and foremost you're a human being. And I'm asking: where is God in your cosmography?
GALILEO: Within ourselves or nowhere.[34]

Galileo plays the defense of "I'm a mathematician" "not a theologian," but the next time he speaks he makes a grand theological statement. The very moment after proclaiming that he is not a theologian, he forgoes any attempt at proving to Sagredo what he is saying through his specialty, mathematics, and immediately creates a narrative of the world, or worldview, outside his area of expertise.

Later in the play, in scene seven, once Galileo is called in front of the Inquisition (after the Vatican research institute proves Galileo's findings, Galileo and Cardinal Bellarmin have a battle of citing Scripture, each using quotes from the bible to prove his own point. But, again, Galileo plays the theologian with an actual theologian. Bellarmin even gives Galileo an out of how he can work on his theories: "You are also at liberty to treat the doctrine in question mathematically, in the form of a hypothesis."[35] Galileo tries to out-theologian the theologians. This, of course, is an affront to the theologians who sees someone from a field that threatens the Church. Bellarmin says: "Science is the rightful and much-loved daughter of the Church," but Galileo's narrative, the way he casts it, is intended "to shake men's faith in the Church."[36] Galileo, however, is convinced that his use of reason can triumph over any theological debate. But this is his hubris. Galileo ultimately suffers from an Aristotelian hubris of pride; while ultimately correct, he still displays unhealthy pride in his method of reasoning. This hubris dictates the arc of the play: from the discovery of Galileo's hubris to the trouble it gets him in, and its necessary resolution, but a resolution that leads to knowledge of what he did and that brings him ultimate shame.

When Galileo speaks to the Little Monk in scene eight, after the Little Monk makes a compelling argument as to why "simple people" need religion,[37] the Little Monk poses a question to Galileo, and Galileo's response is quite telling:

THE LITTLE MONK: But don't you think that the truth will get through without us [the Church], so long as it's true?

GALILEO: No, no, no. The only truth that gets through will be what we force through: the victory of reason will be the victory of people who are prepared to reason, nothing else.[38]

Galileo's worldview is a black-and-white, all-or-nothing worldview. While Galileo's goals are admirable, he lets the ideals of science overtake the realities of his society. Galileo is the scientific version of Henrik Ibsen's religious Brand. Trying to jam a black-and-white worldview down the throats of the unwilling or the unable only leads to being ostracized and isolated (ultimately experienced by both Brand and Galileo).

Karl Korsch, a member (importantly, in my opinion) of the Fabian Society, was Brecht's teacher. Brecht specifically went to Korsch, one of the leading German Marxist scholars, to teach him Marxism. Douglas Kellner writes at length about how Brecht used a Korschian version of the Marxian dialectic in both his aesthetic theory and practice.[39] Unlike bourgeois political economy and theory that dealt with forms of bourgeois society in universal, eternal, and unchanging terms, Korsch viewed Marxism through Marx's analysis of historically distinct and specific features of capitalism and bourgeois society with a method that could analyze distinct social formations critically and transform them radically: a Marxian dialectic, then, is a critical dialectic that sees reality as a process of continual change and focuses on the contradictions and antagonisms that make transformation possible.[40] Kellner suggests that both Brecht's epic theater and his "learning plays" could be understood in terms of Korschian Marxism. In his epic theater, built on Korsch's view of Marxian principles of historical specification and critique, Brecht aimed to show the audience the historically specific features of an environment with the goal of showing how that environment influenced, shaped, and very often "battered and destroyed the characters."[41] In Brecht's later type of theatre, *Lehrstück* ("learning play"), which *Life of Galileo* falls under, Brecht described these plays as "a collective political meeting" with active audience participation that were modeled on Korsch's view that correct doctrine and practice should be discovered and carried out by participatory, collective practices (i.e., how Korsch envisioned workers' councils operating) instead of hierarchical manipulation and domination.[42]

While Korsch clearly made his own impact on and contributions to Marxist theory, I think it is important—whether or not Brecht was directly influenced by it—that Korsch was a member of the Fabian Society. The Fabian Society, from its founding in 1884 to its present-day organization as a "think tank," has worked through intellectual critique and has espoused the notion of socialism by gradual, not revolutionary, means. And while we observe everything that Kellner suggests of Korsch's view of Marxism in *Galileo*, I also believe that, fundamentally, Korsch is the influence (whether direct or indirect) on the Fabian Society. The tragedy of the play is, ultimately, put in terms of a contradiction. However, this tragedy can be explored in light of the Fabian Society (not just Korsch). While Galileo is absolutely right in everything he argues, his pride (hubris) in his own reason and the method of reason allows him to lose sight of the one narrative he can persuasively create (a mathematical understanding of the universe); instead, he is a man (and a method) not of his society—attempting a radical overthrow of the social order (associated with revolutionary Marxism) and not being content with a step-by-step approach (an approach advocated by the Fabian Society)—who literally and figuratively ends up no longer a part of his society (winding up in exile). Galileo's tragedy—similar to Ibsen's Brand, but unlike *Brand*, *Galileo* is historically specific—is his all-or-nothing *telos*-approach in a specific society (early-seventeenth-century Italy) that could not and did not want to hear the specific message Galileo was trying to send (i.e., the earth was not the center of the universe, a fact in conflict with biblical teachings).

Galileo's quest or the love of technology

Bruno Latour and Brecht

Two different productions that appear in *Theatre Journal* set up my conclusions about *Galileo*. A review of the play in 1981, staged by the Pittsburgh Public Theatre and Buhl Planetarium (directed by J. Ranelli), is notable not for what the production was able to accomplish but for precisely the points that the reviewer, Albert E. Kalson, noticed were missing:

> The ambiguous final scene of the final version, in which Andrea smuggles Galileo's writings out of the country, frequently cut, is enacted in the Pittsburgh Public version (the program unforgivably credits no adaptor/translator), but its significance is not clear in the production itself. In fact one may search in vain through the usual published versions of the play for that significance, but needs finally to rely on critic Eric Bentley for what the author himself has failed to point up in the work: "The play abuts upon the

Marxist realization that the people must learn not to rely on the Great Men of the bourgeoisie for their salvation: they will have to save themselves." The Pittsburgh Public's performance of the final scene does not evoke a necessary contrast with the earlier carnival scene; thus it fails to make the point that a once enlightened populace embracing the freedom of knowledge, albeit briefly, has been thrust again into the darkness of superstition and tradition.[43]

Here, the reviewer shows how the production's lack of (what I translate Bentley as saying is) a specifically-Korschian view of Marxism does not do the play justice, ultimately "fail[ing] to make the point." Thus, while the director of the Pittsburgh Public's production is not that successful, its reasons for failure raise the very questions that this chapter brings up.

In 1988, The New Rose Theatre in Portland, Oregon, put on *The Life of Galileo* with Howard Brenton's translation. Rachel B. Shteir, the reviewer, notes in tremendous detail how the director, Heinz-Uwe Haus, created a production that was "alive with contradictions within and between characters, between ideas and feelings, intentions and behaviors," which to Shteir captured the "vitality" of this production,[44] but it was Shteir's interpretation of how the character of Galileo was played that was the most noteworthy: "Galileo, as played by Shabaka from the San Fransisco Mime Troupe, is not a Renaissance Faust type but rather a modern scientist-engineer, caught in a bind between indulging himself in what he likes to do best and the social consequences of his discoveries and actions."[45]

To further explore these two productions and how they relate to my reading of *Galileo*, I would like to develop a working parallel with the sociologist Bruno Latour's book, *Aramis or the Love of Technology* (1996). Latour's book, written as a postmodern detective novel composed of a bricolage of narratives and documents, investigates a large-scale urban engineering project to create an adaptable guided-transport system in Paris called Aramis that started in 1971 and died in 1987. Based upon the relatively simple technology of electronic coupling, individual cars (holding just a few people) would, in theory, be able to link together and separate at appropriate times in order to pick up people not on the main subway lines from vast outer territories in Paris and deliver them directly to downtown Paris. After years of prototypes and tests, the project ultimately died. Latour concludes that the scientists and engineers fell in love with the technology, with its *ideal* potential, ignoring the realities of the world: "Aramis had not incorporated any of the transformations of its environment. It had remained purely an object, a pure object. Remote from the social arena, remote from history; intact."[46] In a large sense, this is Korsch's rebuttal to bourgeois political economy and theory (and this is the rebuttal that is missing in Ranelli's production): in order to affect change, we cannot deal with universals (controlled by a hierarchical bourgeoisie) but we need to learn from specific historical moments (in order to create a proletariat revolution). Thus, Brecht's Galileo, while espousing the ideals of science and reason (and having the contradictions of social disharmony presented through Galileo's situation), is fallible and destined to be "battered and destroyed" because Galileo operates in and creates a narrative of universal reason (and justice). Brecht, in creating a modern history play about Galileo, has created a character that mirrors the Marxists that Korsch criticized for their lack of taking specific historical "conditions" into account. While Brecht's Galileo is noble for his pursuit of an ideal (and a noble ideal at that), just like bourgeois political economy and theory, Galileo fell in love with an idea/ideal, with a technology (i.e., the telescope), with a method (i.e., scientific reason), none of which were *adapted* to meet the reality of the conditions of Galileo's society; most importantly, *Galileo could not adapt his narrative to his specific audience*. Just like one of the most ambitious technological projects the world has even seen in Aramis, Galileo's project initially fails. This is, in a large sense, the Galileo that was created in Haus' production.

But as I opened the close reading of this play in this chapter with the statement that Brecht wants us to remember that there are perfect systems even in larger imperfect ones, the fact that the play ends with Andrea and the copy of Galileo's manuscript, *Discoursi*, "cross[ing] the Italian frontier,"[47] suggests that a narrative *can* exist that will change the world. Andrea, in the second to last scene, understands the *narrative* that Galileo could never seem to create: "Science makes only one demand: contribution to science."[48] Such *discoursi* do exist to change the world, but like Galileo's final book (unlike Galileo during his life) the *Discoursi* is grounded in specifics and written appropriately for a specific audience (i.e., a scientific text for scientists). This is what the audience must take away; this is the manner in which Brecht instructs the audience to redirect their *telos* and look at their own society, translating—more effectively than Galileo—the narrative of a historically specific condition to the proletariat. Brecht's *Galileo*, then, written in Brecht's most un-Brechtian-like form, is, paradoxically, Brecht's *magnum opus* on his own political and social theories for radical change.

Notes

1. Brecht, *Life of Galileo*, , 6.
2. Ibid. 8.
3. Brecht, "Short Organum," 193.
4. Ibid. 195.
5. I first present an argument like this in my discussion of Eugene O'Neill's "sea plays," where I argue that O'Neill presents two narratives—the narrative of naturalism and the narrative of realism—that each destroy the other, forcing the audience to adopt and create a new worldview: see Bennett "Epistemological Crises,", 97–111
6. MacIntyre, *The Tasks of Philosophy*, 3.
7. Ibid. 4–5.
8. Beckley, "History and Heroism," 56.
9. Ibid. 57.
10. Ibid.
11. Ibid.
12. Dial, "Brecht's Dialectical Dramatics," 8.
13. Ibid. 9.
14. Ibid.
15. Ibid. 10.
16. Ibid.
17. Ibid. 12.
18. See Dial, "Brecht's Dialectical Dramatics"; Cohen, "History and Moral," 115–128; and Weber, "*The Life of Galileo*," 60–78.
19. See Beckley, "History and Heroism"; Dial, "Brecht's Dialectical Dramatics"; and Ellis, "Brecht's *Life of Galileo*," 236–243.
20. See Turner, "*Life of Galileo*," 143–159; Kruger, "Theater Translation as Reception," 34–47.
21. "Telescope," Lynd, *The Class-Book of Etymology*.
22. "Telos," *Oxford English Dictionary*, 2nd ed., 1989.
23. Brecht, *Galileo* 6.
24. Brecht, *Galileo* 8.
25. Weber 62.
26. Ibid.
27. John Willett and Ralph Manheim, "Introduction," Bertolt Brecht, *Life of Galileo*, Trans. John Willett, Eds. John Willett and Ralph Manheim (New York: Arcade Publishing, 1994), xix.
28. Ibid.
29. Brecht, *Life of Galileo*, 5.
30. Ibid. 5–8.
31. Sohlich, "The Dialectic of Mimesis," 52.

32 Ibid. 24.
33 Ibid. 25.
34 Ibid. 28.
35 Ibid. 60.
36 Ibid.
37 Ibid. 65–66.
38 Ibid. 68.
39 Kellner, "Brecht's Marxist Aesthetic," 29.
40 Ibid. 30.
41 Ibid. 31.
42 Ibid. 34.
43 Kalson, Review of *The Life of Galileo* and *There's a Message for you from the Man in the Moon*, 535.
44 Shteir, Review of *The Life of Galileo*, 100.
45 Ibid.
46 Latour, *Aramis*, , 280.
47 Brecht, *Life of Galileo*, 110.
48 Ibid. 107.

Conclusion:
For All Seasons—The Particulars and the Universals of Man in Bolt's *A Man for All Seasons*

Abstract: *The Conclusion examines how the post–WWII play,* A Man for All Seasons, *is both similar and departs from the other plays discussed in this book. Like the Common Man in Bolt's play, who missed an opportunity to continue to serve under More and give a not guilty verdict to save an innocent life,* A Man for All Seasons *plays upon the feelings of missed opportunities, guilt, and wishing that we (the Common Men, Common Women, and all of humanity) had chosen different paths, slightly more honorable and slightly more self-sacrificing, in order to save even just one more life.* A Man for All Seasons *is not a call to action in the narrative shape of the telos (like the pre–WWII plays,* Danton's Death, Salome, *and* Galileo*), but it is, instead, a narrative that is meant to haunt us and make us rue the choices of the Common Man.*

Bennett, Y. Michael. *Narrating the Past through Theatre: Four Crucial Texts.* New York: Palgrave Macmillan, 2013. DOI: 10.1057/9781137275424.

Conclusion 75

Robert Bolt's *A Man for All Seasons* sits on the precipice of modern and contemporary drama, of modernism and postmodernism. Written first as a radio play (1954) and then as a television play (1957) for the BBC, Bolt finished reworking the play in 1960, when it premiered on stage in London. Bolt's final (theatrical) version, fifteen years after the end of WWII, was staged in a much different world than the worlds of the three versions of Brecht's *Life of Galileo*. In terms of the theatrical world, too, it differed greatly from that during the three versions of *Galileo*: By 1960, Western European theatre could not go back to a theatre pre–*Waiting for Godot* (1952/1953), or before the onslaught of plays that, in 1961, came to be known as the Theatre of the Absurd. Bolt, writing during the heyday of the not-self-conscious movement, if you will, of Absurdism, did not write his modern history play in the structure (or less-structured structure) of the plays by Beckett, Genet, Pinter, and many other playwrights doing similar thing at the time. Bolt, instead, took a Brechtian approach in telling the story of Sir Thomas More on the stage.

While Bolt was clearly influenced by Brechtian theatre, as Arthur Thomas Tees beautifully argues, *A Man for All Seasons* is not just an example of Brechtian epic theatre but of a history play, and a medieval allegory, as well.[1] In my opinion, Tees' article, "The Place of the Common Man: Robert Bolt: *A Man for All Seasons*," which focuses on juxtaposing the minor character, the Common Man, with the main character, More, is somewhat of the end-all-be-all statement on Bolt's play. In this conclusion, I will rely on Tees' understanding of the play in order to discuss how, as a modern history play, we see a continuation of what we saw in the chapters on *Danton's Death*, *Salome*, and *Life of Galileo*, respectively. But I will also show how Bolt's play, while still sitting at the very end (arguably) of the "modern" period in the theatre, has a different conception of history and history's temporal framework. As *A Man for All Seasons* was written entirely after WWII (as well as its initial radio version), Bolt's play does not tell its story in the tense of *always*, with its focus simultaneously on the past, present, and future: history's conception of the *telos* is gone in *A Man for All Seasons*, and as Lorenz suggests (discussed in the Introduction), after WWII, there is a mix of "presentism" and a sense of a "haunting" past that never leaves that is also apparent in this play.

Tees argues that the Common Man and More are philosophical polar opposites. On one side, More, a man of principle, keeps silent about his principle and does not openly speak out against the King, even though

DOI: 10.1057/9781137275424

he is opposed to the Oath and, at the expense of his life, refuses to take it. More is concerned that while going against his own principles (by assenting to the Oath) will save his life, it will lead to him losing self-respect and even his soul.² On the other side, the Common Man has the "principle of expediency": while he likes being More's steward, he will not continue employment after a cut in his wages, nor will he take More's place in jail or risk the King's wrath by giving a not guilty verdict at More's treason trial, even though the Common Man does admire More.³ Tees argues that the Common Man's motto is: "Better a live rat than a dead lion"; this worldview suggests to Tees that if the Common Man were in More's position, he would take the Oath despite his personal beliefs, for the Common Man's concern is the loss of life not loss of self.⁴

The Common Man and More, furthermore, are polar opposites in terms of the plot of the play, as Tees sees it: More is the "non-tragic hero" and the Common Man is the "tragic non-hero."⁵ More is not a tragic hero in the classical sense in that his downfall is not caused by any weakness of *his* character.⁶ When More asks the Common Man to stay on at a reduced pay after More resigned his chancellorship, the Common Man—facing a choice between consistent expedieny and a higher moral standard—chooses expediency (not continuing with the lower paying position); thus, the Common Man, in his own small way, had the chance to become a hero, and his choice not to is, in its own way, tragic.⁷

As mentioned before, Tees argues that *A Man for All Seasons* resembles a history play, a medieval allegory, and a modern Brechtian epic drama. As a history play, Bolt, Tees contends, chooses to carefully reflect history, taking some of More's recorded speeches and using it as dialog in the play, and situating it in a dialog that reflects the transcript of More's trial.⁸ Furthermore, all of the characters are real people from the pages of history, except the Common Man, who—except when he is in the role of a commentator lecturer, stepping out of the frame of the play to address the audience as a narrator-*raisonneur*, becoming a non-historical figure who illustrates the morals of history—Tees suggests is still given a plausible historical role in the framework of the play.⁹ As a medieval morality play, the content is didactic (in that it is a history with a lesson or moral) and two characters, though they are both individualized in Bolt's play, are given general titles instead of specific names (i.e., the King and the Common Man).¹⁰

Conclusion   77

As an example of Brechtian epic drama, *A Man for All Seasons* uses the Common Man much like the chorus-like characters that we see in Brecht's plays (e.g., the water-seller in *The Good Person of Szechwan* and the folk singer in *The Caucasian Chalk Circle*).[11] Also like Brecht's plays, scenery is changed in full view of the audience (and when the scenery cannot be flown in readily, then actors bring in the props in front of the audience); the Common Man—in order to show that this is both a play and that one man plays many parts—changes costumes right in front of the audience; and while Brechtian captions that serve as commentary on the action are not present, the Common Man does, once, hang up a sign to identify the setting.[12]

While Bolt is clearly indebted to Brecht's theatrical devices (and Bolt said as much), Tees also points out how Bolt departs from Brecht, especially with the character of the Common Man. As Tees reminds us, Bolt himself argues that rather than produce estrangement or alienation, the Common Man was intended to be a device to encourage the audience to identify with him and participate in the play.[13] Tees sees one more reason why the Common Man is non-Brechtian: a Brechtian commentator-narrator generally presents the author's own view of the action and its significance, but the Common Man, whether speaking outside the frame of the play (á la Brecht), or serving as a *raisonneur* within the frame of the play, plays the devil's advocate, taking a position and having a philosophy that is the opposite of Bolt (and, thus, this dramatic irony surrounding the Common Man's words and actions works as a substitute for comic relief).[14]

In my view, too, all rests upon the Common Man, however, to extend Tees' final points, and I argue as such to demonstrate how this modern history play, *A Man for All Seasons*, albeit a post-WWII history play, clearly departs from the other modern history plays discussed in the three chapters. In some sense, we see a very clear arc from *Danton's Death* onward towards Brechtian notions of the theatre, particularly notions of alienation. The alienation effect, if you will, found in *Danton's Death*, *Salome*, and *Galileo* are used to force the audience to immediately think about their future actions, bringing the past and present to bear on the future. But as Bolt says himself, he did not want the Common Man to alienate the audience. Instead, the Common Man is much more like Thorton Wilder's Stage Manager in *Our Town* (1938). Yes, *Our Town* is meta-theatrical just like Brechtian epic drama, but the Common Man and the Stage Manager (who also plays many roles and serves as a narrator and commentator) exist in each play, much like in a medieval

DOI: 10.1057/9781137275424

morality play, to represent something of an "everyman," to "transcend history," as Tees suggests about the Common Man.[15] The difference, of course, between *A Man for All Seasons* and *Our Town* is its historical specificity (and the fact that *Our Town* is in no way a history play): Bolt's play is set in literally and figuratively a *historical transcript*; Wilder's play is set in a universal town. But these two characters who reach out to the audience, in effect, allow the audience to be a part of the play, and if they (the Common Man and the Stage Manager) exist in that world, we exist in that world as well. Thus, while *A Man for All Seasons* is historically very specific, and even despite the fact that he takes positions that the audience may see as cowardly and self-serving, the existence of an "everyman" type of character suggests to the audience, not the question that is posed in a Brechtian drama *what if I lived under those circumstances?* but rather, that *it is human nature to want to preserve your own life.*

In some sense, Bolt's More is the very antithesis of Brecht's Galileo: More acts above society's constraints whereas Galileo bends to them. Given that the action *does* revolve around More and not the Common Man, Bolt examines the extraordinary. Whereas Brecht's Galileo is extraordinary in many respects, Galileo is a clear tragic hero with much hubris. Thus, without some sense of alienation, the audience is not forced to use their critical tools to *change* future history, and with More as the main character of *A Man for All Seasons*, the audience, along with the Common Man, become merely onlookers to the tragedies of history.

And it is the sense of the hopeless onlooker (who may have even had a chance to be a hero) that characterizes some of post-WWII drama, maybe most prominently in Harold Pinter's *The Birthday Party* and *The Dumb Waiter*, where in Pinter's aptly named "comedies of menace," the audience is rendered to be a hopeless onlooker, being forced to watch the approaching seeming-doom, without the ability to shout out, *just get out of the room, just get out of there, it is dangerous!* Needless to say, after the horrors of the Holocaust many people must have felt like hopeless onlookers, some of whom may have also had a chance to be a hero, but who (like the Common Man) chose not to in order to save themselves? And like the Common Man, who missed an opportunity to continue to serve under More and give a not guilty verdict to save an innocent life, *A Man for All Seasons* plays upon the feelings of missed opportunities, guilt, and wishing that we (the Common Men, Common Women, and all of humanity) had chosen different paths, slightly more honorable and slightly more self-sacrificing, in order to save even just one more life. *A Man for All Seasons* is not a call to action in the narrative shape of the *telos* (like *Danton's Death*, *Salome*, and *Galileo*), but it is, instead, a narrative that is meant to *haunt* us and make us rue the choices of the Common Man.

Haunting again

To conclude, I want to turn back to Marvin Carlson's *The Haunted Stage* and the word, "again." Carlson suggests that the theatre is a site that presents things "that we have seen before":

> The retelling of stories already told, the reenactment of events already enacted, the reexperience of emotions already experienced, these are and have always been central concerns of the theatre in all times and places, but closely allied to these concerns are the particular production dynamics of theatre: the stories it chooses to tell, the bodies and other physical materials it utilizes to tell them, and the places in which they are told. Each of these production elements are also, to a striking degree, composed of material "that we have seen before," and the memory of that recycled material as it moves through new and different productions contributes in no small measure to the richness and density of the operations of theatre in general as a site of memory, both personal and cultural.[16]

The question, though, in modern history plays such as Büchner's *Danton's Death*, Wilde's *Salome*, and Brecht's *Life of Galileo*, is *have we seen these things before?* In cultural memory, yes, we have "seen before" the history that is presented on the stage in the modern history plays. But can we say the same about our individual memories? Do I remember a time, as was presented in all of the plays in these three chapters, when I lived in a society where the consequences of my choices was either shame (or losing respect for myself because I would go against my principles) or death? Do I *remember* that feeling or position? Fortunately, no.

And, thus, what I see presented on the stage "again," specifically in a modern history play, is not something that *I* can go "back" to or recall. It is something that *I* must encounter "anew." While I know the situations in front of me as I watch a modern history play from a *cultural* standpoint, I am a stranger in a strange land. I cannot harken "back" to my memories to make sense of what I see before me. Familiarity leads to complacency, these playwrights of modern history plays seem to suggest: *always*, I must learn "anew."

Notes

1. Arthur Thomas Tees, "The Place of the Common Man: Robert Bolt: *A Man for All Seasons*," *University Review* 36 (1969): 69.
2. Ibid. 67.
3. Ibid.
4. Ibid.
5. Ibid.
6. Ibid.
7. Ibid. 68.
8. Ibid. 69.
9. Ibid.
10. Ibid.
11. Ibid. 70.
12. Ibid.
13. Ibid.
14. Ibid.
15. Ibid. 69.
16. Marvin Carlson, *The Haunted Stage: The Theatre as Memory Machine* (Ann Arbor: The University of Michigan Press, 2003), 3–4.

Bibliography

"Again," *Oxford English Dictionary*, 2nd ed., 1989.
Albee, Edward. *Who's Afraid of Virginia Woolf?* New York: Signet, 1983.
"Anew," *Oxford English Dictionary*, 2nd ed., 1989.
Assmann, Aleida. *Cultural Memory and Western Civilization: Functions, Media, Archives.* Cambridge: Cambridge UP, 2011.
Bennett, Michael Y. "Brecht in the Wilde: *Salome*'s Liminal Spaces and the Storyteller." *Journal of Theatre and Drama* 7/8 (2001/2002): 145–156.
———. "Epistemological Crises in O'Neill's S. S. *Glencairn* Plays," in Michael Y. Bennett, Benjamin D. and Carson Eugene (eds) *O'Neill's One-Act Plays: New Critical Perspectives.* New York: Palgrave Macmillan, 2012, 97–111.
———. "The Minoritarian Linguist in Translation: *Homebody/Kabul*'s Answer to Deleuze and Guattari" *Rhizomes* 20 (Summer 2010): <http://www.rhizomes.net/issue20/bennett.html>. Last Accessed 22 April 2012.
———. "Review of *Salome: The Reading.*" *Theatre Journal* 56.2 (May 2004): 305–306.
———. "A Wilde Performance: Bunburying and 'Bad Faith' in *Salome* and *The Importance of Being Earnest*," in Michael Y. Bennett (ed.) *Refiguring Oscar Wilde's* Salome Amsterdam: Rodopi, 2011, 167–181.
———. *Words, Space and the Audience: The Theatrical Tension between Empiricism and Rationalism.* New York: Palgrave Macmillan, 2012.

Beckley, Richard J. "History and Heroism in Bertolt Brecht's Historical Plays." *Gestus: A Quarterly Journal of Brechtian Studies* 1.3–4 (1985): 51–61.

Bentley, Michael. "Past and 'Presence': Revisiting Historical Ontology." *History and Theory* 45 (October 2006): 349–361.

Bhabha, Homi. *Nation and Narration*. London: Routledge, 1990.

Brantley, Ben. "Veils or No Veils, Whatever She Wants She Gets." *New York Times*, 1 May 2003: E1 and E5.

Brecht, Bertolt. *Life of Galileo*. Trans. John Willett. Eds. John Willett and Ralph Manheim. New York: Arcade Publishing, 1994.

———. "A Short Organum for the Theatre," in John Willett (ed. and trans.) *Brecht on Theatre: The Development of an Aesthetic*. New York: Hill and Wang, 1964, 179–205.

Büchner, Georg. *Danton's Death*. Trans. Henry J. Schmidt. New York: Bard Books, 1971.

Canning, Charlotte M. and Thomas Postlewait. "Representing the Past: An Introduction on Five Themes," in Charlotte M. Canning and Thomas Postlewait (eds) *Representing the Past: Essays in Performance Historiography*. Iowa City: University of Iowa Press, 2010, 1–34.

Carlson, Marvin. *The Haunted Stage: The Theatre as Memory Machine*. Ann Arbor: The University of Michigan Press, 2003.

———. *Performance: A Critical Introduction*. London: Routledge, 1996.

———. *The Theatre of the French Revolution*. Ithaca: Cornell University Press, 1966.

Carson, Rebecca. "The Transformation of History into Drama: The Women's History Play in America, 1900–1940." *Theatre Studies* 43 (1998): 7–21.

Cavanagh, Dermot. *Language and Politics in the Sixteenth-Century History Play*. New York: Palgrave Macmillan, 2003.

Cave, Richard Allen. "Wilde Designs: Some Thoughts about Recent British Productions of His Plays." *Modern Drama* 37.1 (1994): 175–191.

de Certeau, Michel. *The Writing of History*. Trans. Tom Conley. New York: Columbia UP, 1988.

Cohen, M. A. "History and Moral in Brecht's The Life of Galileo," in Siegfried Mews (ed.) *Critical Essays on Bertolt Brecht*. Boston: Hall, 1989, 115–128.

Craig, Edward Gordon. *On the Art of the Theatre*. Chicago: Browne's Bookstore, 1911.

Crowley, Tony. "Memory and Forgetting in a Time of Violence: Brian Friel's Meta-History Plays." *Estudios Irelandeses* 3 (2008): 72–83.
Devenyi, Jutka. "Consciousness and Structure in *Danton's Death*." *Journal of Dramatic Theory and Criticism* 10.1 (Fall 1995): 43–57.
Dial, Joseph. "Brecht's Dialectical Dramatics as Political Praxis," *CLIO* 11.1 (1981): 7–13.
Diamond, Elin. "Modern Drama/Modernity's Drama," *Modern Drama* 44.1 (Spring 2001): 3–15.
Dillon, Janet. "The Early Tudor History Play," in Teresa Grant and Barbara Ravelhofer (eds) *English Historical Drama, 1500–1660: Forms Outside the Canon*. Basingstoke: Palgrave Macmillan, 2008, 32–57.
Donohue, Joseph. "*Salome* and the Wildean Art of Symbolist Theatre." *Modern Drama* 37.1 (1994): 84–103.
Ellis, Leslie. "Brecht's *Life of Galileo* as an Aristotelian Tragedy," in Helmut Hal Rennert (ed.) *Essays on Twentieth-Century German Drama and Theater: An American Reception, 1977–1990*. New York: Peter Lang, 2004, 236–243
Ellmann, Richard. *Oscar Wilde*. New York: Alfred A. Knopf, 1988.
———. *Oscar Wilde at Oxford*. Washington: Library of Congress, 1984.
Favorini, Attilio. "History, Collective Memory, and Aeschylus' *The Persians*." *Theatre Journal* 55 (2003): 99–111.
———. *Memory at Play: From Aeschylus to Sam Shepard*. New York: Palgrave Macmillan, 2008.
Fischer, Carol A. "Dramatic Time: Phenomena and Dilemmas." *Study of Time* 13 (2010): 241–256.
Fischer, Gerhard. "Playwrights Playing with History: The Play within the Play and German Historical Drama (Büchner, Brecht, Weiss, Müller)." *The Play within the Play: The Performance of Meta-Theatre and Self-Reflection*. Amsterdam: Rodopi, 2007, 249–265.
Griffin, Benjamin. "The Birth of the History Play: Saint, Sacrifice, and Reformation." *SEL* 39.2 (Spring 1999): 217–237.
Halperin-Royer, Ellen. "Robert Wilson and the Actor: Performing in *Danton's Death*," in Phillip B. Zarrilli (ed.) *Acting (Re)Considered: A Theoretical and Practical Guide*. 2nd ed. London: Routledge, 2002, 319–333.
Hammond, Brean S. "'Is Everything History?': Churchill, Barker, and the Modern History Play." *Comparative Drama* 41.1 (Spring 2007): 1–23.

Hattaway, Michael. "The Shakespearean History Play," in Michael Hattaway (ed.) *The Cambridge Companion to Shakespeare's History Plays*. Cambridge: Cambridge UP, 2002, 3–24.

Hoenselaars, A. J. "Shakespeare and the Early Modern **History Play**," in Michael Hattaway (ed.) *The Cambridge Companion to Shakespeare's History Plays*. Cambridge: Cambridge UP, 2002, 25–40.

Hunter, G. K. "Notes on the Genre of the History Play," In John W. Velz (ed.) *Shakespeare's English Histories: A Quest for Form and Genre*. New York: Medieval & Renaissance Texts & Studies, 1996, 229–240.

———. "Truth and Art in History Plays." *Shakespeare Survey* 42 (1990): 15–24.

Ibsen, Henrik. "To the Norwegian Students, September 10, 1874." *Speeches and New Letters*. Trans. Arne Kildal. Boston: Richard G. Badger, 1910, 48–52.

Jones, Swann. *The Fairy Tale: The Magic Mirror of Imagination*. New York: Twayne Publishers, 1995.

Kalson, Albert E. "Review of *The Life of Galileo* and *There's a Message for you from the Man in the Moon*." *Theatre Journal* 33.4 (December 1981): 535–537.

Kastan, David Scott. "The Shape of Time: Form and Value in the Shakespearean History Play." *Comparative Drama* 7 (1973): 259–277.

Kellner, Douglas. "Brecht's Marxist Aesthetic: The Korsch Connection," in Betty Nance Weber and Hubert Heinen (eds) *Bertolt Brecht: Political Theory and Literary Practice*. Athens: University of Georgia Press, 2010, 29–42.

Kelly, Katherine E. "Review of *Danton's Death*." *Theatre Journal* 45.3 (October 1993): 375–377.

Kewes, Paulina. "The Elizabethan History Play: A True Genre?" in Richard Dutton and Jean E. Howard (eds) *A Companion to Shakespeare's Works, Volume II: The Histories*. Malden: Blackwell, 2006, 170–193.

Knezevic, Dubravka. "Marked with Red Ink." *Theatre Journal* 48.4 (1996): 407–418.

Kohl, Norbert. *Oscar Wilde: The Works of a Conformist Rebel*. Trans. David Henry Wilson. Cambridge: Cambridge University Press, 1989.

Kruger, Loren. "Theater Translation as Reception: The Example of Brecht's *Galileo*." *Communications from the International Brecht Society* 14.2 (1985): 34–47.

Kurtz, Martha A. "Rethinking Gender and Genre in the History Play." *SEL* 36.2 (Spring 1996): 267–287.

Latour, Bruno. *Aramis or the Love of Technology.* Trans. Catherine Porter. Cambridge: Harvard University Press, 1999.

Lorenz, Chris. "Unstuck in Time. Or: The Sudden Presence of the Past," in Karin Tilmans, Frank Van Vree, and Jay Winter (eds) *Performing the Past: Memory, History, and Identity in Modern Europe.* Amsterdam: Amsterdam UP, 2010, 67–102.

Lynd, James. *The Class-Book of Etymology: Designed to Promote Precision in the Use, and Facilitate the Acquisition of a Knowledge of the English Language.* Philadelphia: E. C. & J. Biddle, 1848.

MacDonald, Ian Andrew. "Oscar Wilde as a French Writer: Considering Wilde's French in *Salomé*," in Michael Y. Bennett (ed.) *Refiguring Oscar Wilde's Salome.* Amsterdam: Rodopi, 2011, 1–19.

MacIntyre, Alasdair. *The Tasks of Philosophy: Selected Essays, Volume 1.* Cambridge: Cambridge UP, 2006.

Marx, Karl. *The Eighteenth Brumaire of Louis Bonaparte.* New York: International Publishers, 1998.

McAuley, Gay. *Space in Performance: Making Meaning in the Theatre.* Ann Arbor: University of Michigan Press, 1999.

Müller, Harro. "Identity, Paradox, Difference Conceptions of Time in the Literature of Modernity." *MLN* 111.3 (1996): 523–532.

Murray, Alex. "Acquiescing into a Facile Orthodoxy?: Wilde, Pater and the Politics of Cultural Parallax." *Irish Studies Review* 13.3 (2005): 325–332.

Nassaar, Christopher S. "Wilde's *The Happy Prince and Other Tales* and *A House of Pomegranates*." *The Explicator* 60.3 (Spring 2002): 142–145.

Nietzsche, Friedrich. *The Use and Abuse of History.* Trans. Adrian Collins. New York: Macmillan Publishing Company, 1957.

"Penumbra". *The Oxford English Dictionary.* 1997 ed.

Quigley, Austin E. "Realism and Symbolism in Oscar Wilde's *Salomé*." *Modern Drama* 37.1 (1994): 104–119.

Richardson, Brian. " 'Time is Out of Joint': Narrative Models and the Temporality of the Drama." *Poetics Today* 8.2 (1987): 299–309.

Robinson, Marsha S. *Writing the Reformation: Actes and Monuments and the Jacobean History Play.* Aldershot: Ashgate, 2002.

Robyns, Clem. "Translation and Discursive Identity." *Poetics Today* 15.3 (Fall 1994): 405–428.

Rokem, Freddie. "Narratives of Armed Conflict and Terrorism in the Theatre: Tragedy and History in Hanoch Levin's Murder." *Theatre Journal* 54.4 (2002): 555–573.

Rokem, Freddie. *Performing History: Theatrical Representations of the Past in Contemporary Theatre*. Iowa City: University of Iowa Press, 2000.

Runia, Eelco. "Burying the Dead, Creating the Past." *History and Theory* 46 (October 2007): 313–325.

Shortslef, Emily. "Acting as an Epitaph: Performing Commemoration in the Shakespearean History Play." *Critical Survey* 22.2 (2010): 11–24.

Shteir, Rachel B. "Review of *The Life of Galileo*." *Theatre Journal* 41.1 (March 1989): 99–101.

Smith, Philip. "Narrating the Guillotine: Punishment Technology as Myth and Symbol." *Theory, Culture & Society* 20.5 (2003): 27–51.

Sohlich, Wolfgang. "The Dialectic of Mimesis and Representation in Brecht's *Life of Galileo*," *Theatre Journal* 45 (1993): 49–64.

Spencer, Jenny. "Performing Translation in Contemporary Anglo-American Drama." *Theatre Journal* 59 (2007): 389–410.

"Stay." *Oxford English Dictionary*, 2nd ed., 1989.

Tanitch, Robert. *Oscar Wilde on Stage and Screen*. London: Methuen, 1999.

Tees, Arthur Thomas. "The Place of the Common Man: Robert Bolt: *A Man for All Seasons*." *University Review* 36 (1969): 67–71.

"Telos." *Oxford English Dictionary*, 2nd ed., 1989.

Tillis, Steve. "The Actor Occluded: Puppet Theatre and Acting Theory." *Theatre Topics* 6.2 (1996): 109–119.

"Translate." *Oxford English Dictionary*, 2nd ed., 1989.

"Translator." *Oxford English Dictionary*, 2nd ed., 1989.

Turner, Cathy. "*Life of Galileo*: Between Contemplation and the Command to Participate," in Peter Thomson (ed.) *The Cambridge Companion to Brecht*. Cambridge: Cambridge UP, 2006, 143–159.

Ullyot, Michael. "Seneca and the Early Elizabethan History Play," in Teresa Grant and Barbara Ravelhofer (eds) *English Historical Drama, 1500-1660: Forms Outside the Canon*. Basingstoke: Palgrave Macmillan, 2008, 98–124.

de Vries, Kees. "Intertextuality and Intermediality in Oscar Wilde's *Salome* or: How Oscar Wilde became a Postmodernist," in Michael Y. Bennett (ed.) *Refiguring Oscar Wilde's* Salome. Amsterdam: Rodopi, 2011, 235–255.

Weber, Betty Nance. "*The Life of Galileo* and the Theory of Revolution in Permanence," in Betty Nance Weber and Hubert Heinen (eds) *Bertolt Brecht: Political Theory and Literary Practice*. Athens: University of Georgia Press, 2010, 60–78

Weineck, Silke-Maria. "Sex and History, or Is there an Erotic Utopia in *Datons Tod*?" *The German Quarterly* 73.4 (Fall 2000): 351–365.

White, Hayden. *The Content of the Form: Narrative Discourse and Historical Representation*. Baltimore: The John Hopkins University Press, 1987.

Wilde, Oscar. *The Complete Letters of Oscar Wilde*. Eds Merlin Holland and Rupert Hart-Davis. New York: Henry Holt and Company, 2000.

———. "Salome," in Peter Raby (ed.) *Oscar Wilde: The Importance of Being Earnest and Other Plays*. Oxford: Oxford University Press, 2008, 61–91.

Willett, John and Ralph Manheim. "Introduction," Bertolt Brecht. *Life of Galileo*. Trans. John Willett. Eds. John Willett and Ralph Manheim. New York: Arcade Publishing, 1994, vi–xxii.

Wirth, Andrzej. "The Thrust Stage as Guillotine." *Performing Arts Journal* 15.1 (January 1993): 59–61.

Zipes, Jack. *Fairy Tale as Myth: Myth as Fairy Tale*. Kentucky: University Press of Kentucky, 1994.

Index

"Again", 2–4, 79
Always (tense of), 3–4, 10, 24, 75, 79
Anderson, Mary, 44
"Anew", 2–4, 9, 16, 79
Antiquities of the Jews, 38, 53
Assmann, Aleida, 12–14

"Back", 2–4, 9, 16, 79
Beckley, Richard J., 61
Bennett, Michael Y., 5
Bhabha, Homi, 15
Blau, Herbert, 2
Brown, Peter, 8

Canning, Charlotte M., 6
Carlson, Marvin, 2, 79
Certeau, Michel de, 7, 12, 46, 60
"Chronicle", 6, 11

Devenyi, Jutka, 32–33
Dial, Joseph, 61–62
Diamond, Elin, 8, 12
Donohue, Joseph, 3, 38

Favorini, Attilio, 12–13

Griffin, Benjamin, 8, 10–11

Halperin-Royer, Ellen, 31
Haunting, 2, 75, 79
Homebody/Kabul, 5
Hunter, G. K., 11

Ibsen, Henrik, 15, 24
The Importance of Being Earnest, 42, 53

Kalson, Albert E., 69
Kastan, David Scott, 11
Kelly, Katherine E., 32
Knezevic, Dubravka, 23
Kohl, Norbert, 38, 45
Korsch, Karl, 68–71

Latour, Bruno, 70
Lorenz, Chris, 10

MacDonald, Ian Andrew, 39, 50
MacIntyre, Alasdair, 61
Mahaffy, J. P., 51
Manheim, Ralph, 64
Marius the Epicurean, 51–52
Memory, 2, 8–9, 11–16, 24–26, 79
Murray, Alex, 52

Narrative, 3–4, 6, 8–9, 13, 24, 34, 46–47, 60–61, 65–67, 71, 79
Nassaar, Christopher S., 51–52, 64
Nietzsche, Friedrich, 14

Pater, Walter, 51–52
Performance, 29–31
Postlewait, Thomas, 6

Quigley, Austin, 38

Robyns, Clem, 7–8
Rokem, Freddie, 2–3
Runia, Eelco, 15

Salome: The Reading, 48–49
Shakespeare, William, 2, 12–13
Shteir, Rachel B., 70
Smith, Philip, 29
States, Bert, 2
Strindberg, August, 24

Tees, Arthur Thomas, 75–77
Telos, 4, 10, 46, 62–63, 71, 75, 79

"Transcript", 6–8
"Translate", 4, 32, 34
Translation, 3–5, 24–25, 38–39, 50–51, 65
Translator, 3–4, 7, 65

Weber, Betty Nance, 63–64
White, Hayden, 6, 46, 60
Willett, John, 64
Wilson, Robert, 31–32
Wirth, Andrzej, 31
Who's Afraid of Virginia Woolf? 9
Woyzeck, 44

Zipes, Jack, 45

Printed in the USA
CPSIA information can be obtained
at www.ICGtesting.com
LVHW091503171223
766698LV00004B/331